MW01064528

Miracles Out of Somewhere

by Kerry Livgren

This book is dedicated to my friend, Pastor Rob Raynor, without whose persistence I may not have gotten around to writing it all down.

ISBN: 978-0-578-73566-5

www.numavox.com

Pre-Ramble

This book is a collection of various memories and recollections. They are quite random, ranging from my early childhood, to "advanced" adulthood. Some of them deal with my many experiences with the band "Kansas." Others are just my personal life experiences. Frankly, these stories are things that I consider to be miraculous, or nearly miraculous. Regarding their status as miracles, you must judge for yourself. I apologize for any inaccuracies or omissions, but everything I have written is exactly as I remember it.

I have been blessed to live a remarkable life, or at least it seems so to me. Hopefully, it will serve some greater purpose, and you will derive some enjoyment from reading these stories.

Kerry Livgren

Front Cover Photo by Joe del Tufo, Moonloop Photography

Chapters

Adventures in the Big Apple

The Taxi cabs we were riding in pulled up in front of the Ramada Inn at 48th and 8th Avenue, New York City. To us, it may as well have been the Waldorf. The Ramada was just fine for us. We were in New York to record our first album at the Record Plant! I had repeatedly seen the name of that Studio on many of my album covers – and some very famous bands indeed. This recording session would be the realization of an almost impossible dream. Our band, coming from the Heartland of America, were here to record our own music. Of course the whole story began in Kansas. It was in the early Summer of 1973 in Dodge City when we received the phone call. We had been playing a week's stand at a club there, making just enough money to make it worthwhile. During a break, the bartender informed us that we had someone on the phone from New York. I think it was Dave who answered it. It was Buster Newman – our mysterious contact who had been "Working the Labels" for us in New York City. We had never met the man. In fact, to this day we have never again had contact with him, but were are very grateful that we got his phone call that night in Dodge City. He told us that he had delivered our demo tape to Don Kirshner, and that his new Label, Kirshner Records, was possibly interested in the band. They wanted to fly someone out to Kansas to hear us play. If we sounded as good as the demo tape, they intended to sign us. He also told us that his job was through, and that Wally Gold, Kirshner's assistant, would be taking over. Wally flew to Kansas to hear us at the Ellinwood Opera House. A few days later, we signed the Contract. (The rest of the "signing up" story is told in detail in our Documentary, "Miracles Out of Nowhere.")

So here we were in our overalls, staring up at the skyscrapers of the Big Apple. As the Cabs pulled away, our luggage was sitting all over the sidewalk in front of the Hotel. One of the Bellhops began, very enthusiastically, to load our bags onto a big cart. "Don't you worry boys, I'll take care of these!" Not knowing what to do, we looked at each other for a clue. I cannot emphasize too strongly how little we knew about the ways of the world. We had never stayed in a fancy Hotel before, especially in New York City. Assuming that the Bellhops' uniform meant that he worked there, we cautiously watched as he wheeled our luggage inside. We followed him into the elevator. He began, very methodically, to deposit them one by one at the door of our rooms. Then he stood there with his palm out. This was the wrong thing to do with a bunch of guys from Kansas. We were clueless, but he was persistent. Finally, Dave whispered "I think he expects us to pay him." Dave opened his wallet and handed him a dollar bill. (This, by the way, was a very generous tip where we came from.) The Bellhop looked at it incredulously, and said, in some sort of accent that we couldn't identify, "For dee whole Band?" Uncomfortable silence. "Ooo-kay" he said loudly, and stomped off down the hall shaking his head and muttering to himself. We just looked at each other. "What's his problem?" said one of the guys.

For the next few days we were getting oriented, and being evaluated by Kirshner. First, we were taken to his (very large) office building, and introduced. Wally did the introducing. We also found out that Wally would be our Producer. In addition to meeting Don Kirshner, we met his Attorney, Herb Moelis. Although he was very cordial, our impression was that he was a Bulldog that would just as soon bite your head off. Kirshner was very complementary, thanked us for signing the contract, and seemed genuinely glad to meet us. He looked just like he did on TV, except even more groomed. I remember him being amazed, and very concerned that we had no Artist Management. "We'll have to do something about that." He arranged for us to meet with Shep Gordon, who managed Alice Cooper. (We were very impressed, but later Shep said he wasn't interested in us. After Shep's rejection, he hooked us up with Elliot Abbott, who managed Jim Croce. That didn't work out either.) Then he dropped a big official-looking envelope on the desk in front of him, and said "Here you go, boys, here's your $10,000 advance." Eyes grew wide. I remember little else about our first meeting. Somehow, I was elected to be in possession of that check

– not a job I particularly wanted. I asked his attorney about cashing the check, since I had no idea where to go. He told me to take it to Wall Street, where Kirshner's Bank was. (Where else?)

We went back to our Hotel, and all the guys in the band were practically jumping up and down with glee. $10,000! We were all fantasizing how we would spend our share. After a very quick band meeting, we decided that each guy would get a grand, and the rest of it was to pay off any debts we had. (We weren't totally without responsibility!) And now for the cash. After gazing one more time at that amazing check, signed by Don Kirshner, (wish we had taken a picture of it), I was off to the Bank. Thank goodness I had Dave with me. I had told the guys that I was going to be a bit nervous carrying all that cash on the streets of New York, so Dave agreed to come with me. We went outside and the Doorman got us a Cab. "Wall Street, please." A few minutes later and we were there. The lobby of the Bank was spectacular. I had on the typical T-Shirt and jeans, and Dave had on his overalls. Here were a couple of scruffy young guys with shoulder-length hair, who wanted to cash a check on Wall Street. Every eye was on us. Needless to say, the Teller looked a bit nervous. As I handed him the check, he saw Don Kirshner's signature. He looked at me again, and said "I'll be right back." After a short conversation with a man who was obviously a manager, he returned. "How would you like it?" Now I had been instructed to get Traveler's Checks, for obvious reasons. But after finding out how much those were going to cost us, and a quick confirmation from Dave, I said "Cash please, in Hundred Dollar bills. (I had never seen one before!)

The Teller shoved an envelope, with a big bundle of cash in it, in my direction. "Thanks!" I blurted out, and sat down on a bench in the lobby. Dave sat next to me. I quickly discovered that my jeans were not designed to hold ten grand in the pockets. "Dave, you've got to carry some of this. It's too much." "Oh no Kerry, you agreed to get the money!" said Dave. With Dave's reluctance apparent, I stuffed a $5000 roll in my left front pocket, and the other $5000 in the right. It looked ridiculous. The bulges were patently obvious –

you could see them from across the room. "All right, let's get this over with." As we stepped out on the street, Dave spied a New York Subway sign. "Hey Kerry, let's ride the Subway! I've always wanted to, plus we can save that Cab fare!" I remember thinking "Well, no one would ever suspect that I was carrying all this money on the Subway." I agreed to the ride. Once we got on the car, however, I thought different. We saw a number of individuals who, if they had known, probably would have held up (or worse!) these two yokels from Kansas. I was so nervous, the expression on my face was likely a dead giveaway. The Lord was merciful, however, and we made it back to the Ramada Inn.

The guys were all anxiously waiting together in one room, as Dave and I stepped in the door. "Well,,," someone said. "Yippie!!" I yelled as I flung $100 bills at them. That moment was the culmination of years of "eating dirt." Every face was smiling. No more "a dollar a day" ration, as we had been living on. We were in the money, or so we thought. After a bit of revelry, Phil and I left for our room. We each had our grand in our wallets. "Kerry, I want to go to that row of Music Stores and buy some new Cymbals." We had seen Manny's, Sam Ash, and others nearby. The thought of going to a Music Store with $1000 was too enticing to say no to, although after thinking about it, I decided to tell Phil that I would be glad to go with him, just to look around. For some reason, I was still nervous about having this much money, and I told Phil what I was thinking. I looked around our "Spartan" room, and my eyes landed on the room's air-conditioner/heater. After inspection, I was able to partially dis-assemble it and found just enough space to hide my $1000. "Pretty good idea, Livo." said Phil. After giving it some thought, he decided to take apart his suitcase, and conceal $600 in the lining. "Pretty good idea, yourself." said I.

We were gone about an hour and a half, buying Cymbals and enjoying "Music Store Wonderland." When we got back to the room, we saw that the beds were made. The maids had been there. Phil looked at his suitcase, and noticed that it didn't look right. He opened it up and gasped. "WHERE'S MY SIX HUNDRED

BUCKS?" We looked at each other. Quickly I checked the heater –
my money was still there. Unable to grasp the concept that someone had stolen his money, a slow realization came to us. Aha! It
was a prank. Rich and Dave's room was right next to ours. Phil
knocked loudly on their door. Entering, he said "All right guys.
Very funny! Where is it?" "Where's what?" said Rich. "My 600
bucks!" Dave and Rich just gave us a blank stare. At the same moment, we all realized what had happened. Phil looked sick. "That
figures." said Dave. We finally make some money and it gets
ripped off the first day." We called the Front desk immediately, but
the Hotel vouched for their maids and of course assumed no re-
sponsibility. They called the NYPD. They sent a Uniformed Offi-
cer, and a Detective to our room. These two were right out of a
Movie, with their Manhattan accent. They were not exactly help-
ful. "You mean yous'e guys didn't put the money in the Hotel
Safe?" They told us that there were at least a dozen drug addicts
and other criminals down on the street with keys to the rooms. This
wasn't Kansas, it was New York. They got Phil's information, and
left. We felt so bad for Phil that we took $600 from the stash to pay
bills, and replaced his money.

The next day held better things. Wally called and gave us directions to the Studio – but not the Record Plant. He said this place
was for a rehearsal. Hmm... It was a small, even tiny Recording
room. Wally wanted us to start by recording "Lonely Wind." We
were kind of bummed that it wasn't the Record Plant, but it was
still a Studio in New York. After a short session, it quickly became
evident that it was really not a "rehearsal." We were being evaluated. Apparently Kirshner wanted to make sure that we were capa-
ble of recording before he spent his money in a Studio that cost ten
times as much. After recording successfully, Wally told us that the
next day we would begin working at the Record Plant. Hooray! We
went back to our Hotel in search of lunch. Across the street, there
was a little Restaurant attached to a cheap looking Hotel called
"The President." Phil, Dave, Rich and I decided to check it out. We
walked into the little dining room and sat down. A man, of Middle
Eastern origin, came out from behind the counter and began smil-

ing and speaking to us. "Hello, boys, hello! Welcome! We have some nice lamb today!" He abruptly turned, and shouted though a small window in the wall, "Three Lamb!" He then disappeared. We sat there for a second. Laughing, I said "What just happened?" "I don't know," said Phil. "I think we just ordered!" About a minute later he re-appeared carrying three plates of steaming Lamb, with some sort of orange-colored sauce. "Nice Lamb!" he exclaimed. The surprising thing was – it was delicious! Truly, we were not in Kansas any more. When we finished eating, as we were paying our bill, I noticed a cookie-like pastrie in the glass case. "What is that?" I asked our host. "Oh, that is a Macaroon! You try?" I did. Also delicious. This place became one of our regular eateries, despite the lack of a Menu. It got to where he would call out "Three Lamb!" as we came in the door – followed by a Macaroon, of course.

At last we came to the Studio of our dreams – The Record Plant. Jimi Hendrix, John Lennon, The Allman Brothers, Three Dog Night, and many others had all recorded in these "hallowed halls," and now Kansas was here. We were introduced to our Engineer, Dan Turbeville. Very nice guy. I remember once that he invited Robby and I over to his apartment. He set a tray of some sort of sticky brown substance in front of us, and then scooped some of it up and began eating it. "What is that?" I asked. "Hummus. Haven't you ever seen Hummus?" "Well, we're from Kansas." I answered. He laughed. Running the 24-track recorder was Jimmy "Shoes" Iovine. His nickname came from the outlandish shoes he wore. (Those 70's platforms.) Years later, he would become a very successful Producer. Later, Wally started by going over some of the procedures for our recording sessions. We were in Studio B, and we had to alternate with, of all people, Yoko Ono. Every day we had to tear down our gear, and set up all over again the next. We began to set up the first day, when Wally said "Oh, by the way, you cannot use those Marshall amps in the studio. Nobody records with those. They are just too loud. You can use our amps." Rich and I were stunned. I looked to Dan Turbeville for confirmation. He just shrugged, as if to say "What the Producer says, is what we have to do." The Studio amps were tiny little Fenders. I remember thinking to myself "Jimi Hendrix, The Allman Brothers – *they* used these little Fenders to get those amazing sounds?" Well, Rich and I didn't know any better, so on the first Kansas album we used little Fenders.

Curiously, I don't remember much about the actual recording we did. I do remember that we were all a bit nervous, at least at first anyway. We had some amateur demo recording experience, but we got used to being professionals pretty quickly. Since multi-track overdubs were rudimentary then, you pretty much had to do a whole song from the beginning when recording. I was terrified of making a mistake. Songs like "Apercu" and "Journey from Mariabronn" were especially difficult. Wally just calmly said "Let's try it again." The whole band liked him had a good relationship with him. At one point he called me into this little cubicle he had in his office, which was his "listening room." "Put these on and listen to this." he said. He pulled out a pair of headphones and an LP of Mahler's 8th Symphony, and set the needle on the Finale. "I think you will like this." I thought I knew my composers, but I had never heard Mahler. He bowled me over. His 8th Symphony is a true, and very transcendent masterpiece. I will forever be thankful that he made me aware of Mahler's music. Wally had the unique ability to ascertain anyone's musical interests. As a Producer, he also had the ability to diffuse an argument – in the most diplomatic way possible. I do vividly recall a conversation we had. He pulled me aside one day and said "Kerry, can I talk to you about one of your songs?" "Uh-oh." I thought. "Here it comes. He's going to pull one of my songs off the album." Thankfully, that wasn't it. "About 'Parsichine.'" he said. "What does that title mean to you?" ("Parsichine" was the original title of "Apercu.") "Nothing, really. It's just a fictitious word I made up." (Whenever I couldn't think of a good song title, I was in the habit of just naming the song with a totally original word. Kansas had several such titles.) "Well," said Wally. We've already got 'Belexes', and virtually nobody is going to know what 'Journey from Mariabronn' means, so what would you think of 'Apercu' for a title? In French it means insight." Normally I would bristle at anyone attempting to change one of my songs, but Wally was so persuasive that I couldn't argue with him. "OK by me." I said. I didn't even know any French.

At the Record Plant, there were famous people coming and going all the time. We stood behind Alice Cooper at the Coke machine. (It had ripped him off!) Aerosmith was in Studio A. We never saw them, but I peeked in the door once and saw big amplifiers. (Hmmm...I thought you couldn't record with those.) On one occasion, we met Rick Derringer who was working in another room with Johnny Winter. He invited us to record hand claps on one of their tracks, which we gladly did. Our first outside session! On a typical day, when we were finished recording, we would sometimes walk back to the Hotel. Steve and Robby liked to stop at Smiler's Delicatessen. You could get some good (cheap) stuff to eat there, but I preferred "Haute Cuisine." (The truth is, I wouldn't have known it if it came up and bit me.) On one night, I had a date to impress. She was a nice young lady who I had met in the lobby. Like myself, she was new to New York, so I asked her out to dinner and she accepted. I wanted very much to impress her, so I couldn't exactly take her across the street to Smiler's. I had my eye on this place on 44th St. called Mamma Leone's. Obviously Italian, it was richly decorated to boot. We marched up to the entrance, and presented ourselves. "Do you have a reservation?" asked the Host. (in Topeka, Kansas you never needed one.) "Uh, no, we don't." "I'll see what I can do." In a few seconds he came back and said "Follow me, sir." Seated at a table, we were given two enormous Menus. A Waiter appeared, and asked if I wanted to see the Wine list. "Uh, no thanks." He looked kind of peeved, and left us. I glanced at my date, and she had the faintest look of disappointment on her face. "Really?" I thought. "You wanted wine?" The last time I had tasted wine was High School Graduation night. MD 20/20. Not a pleasant memory. The longer I looked at the Menu, the more I began to get nervous. I didn't recognize a single thing! To me, Italian food meant Spaghetti. That was pretty much it. Not wanting to appear ignorant, and looking for a clue, I asked my date "Well, what are you having?" She told me, but I was no better off.

I couldn't even repeat what she just said. Back to the Menu. Suddenly, I noticed what this meal was going to cost me. Yikes! I began looking for the cheapest thing, but I remembered that I had a thousand dollars to spend. Oh, well. When the Waiter asked me what I wanted to order, I just pointed at the first thing my finger landed on. It was Calamari. "Excellent!" said the Waiter and left the table. (As I write this, I find it almost painful. Really, I am *so* much more cultured now than I was then. I have my wife to thank for that!) After some casual conversation, our dishes arrived. The Waiter set my plate in front of me – and I almost gasped. I managed to stifle it. In front of me was some sort of bizarre, gray creature – his eye staring up at me. I recognized tentacles, but I could not identify it. The Waiter must have known something was wrong. "Does the Calamari not please you, sir?" "Oh, it's fine. It looks fine." I lied. I have a strong stomach, and adventurous taste buds – but *this*? As it turned out, my Squid was not too bad, once I found out what it was. My date knew. She said that usually, it is a plate full of tiny little ones, not a single, colossal specimen. She had not seen that before, and of course neither had I. At last, the Waiter brought the bill. Though I had wanted to eat "fancy," I could scarcely bring myself to pay this bill. A lesson learned. I took her back to the Hotel, said goodnight, and retired to my room. The whole time I was haunted by thoughts of that big eye staring back at me.

We had finished our recording sessions, and thoughts turned to mixing. If it had been up to us, we would have spent a lot more time on the tracks, but Wally seemed to be in a hurry. "That's good enough." or "The clock is ticking." I suppose it wasn't his fault. It was his job to watch over Don Kirshner's money. An argument arose over the mix, however. We were not to be present. Flights home had been booked. I was not about to leave the mixing to Wally, or anyone else, for that matter. This was *our* album. I stood my ground. It was finally agreed that Robby and I would stay to mix the album, while the rest of the guys would go home. Our "victory" would be rather hollow – the mixing sessions were even more hurried than our recording was. Very frustrating. After a couple of days we flew home. We had to get acclimated to a Kansas lifestyle again, and "de-New York" ourselves. We had a *very* long wait before our first album was finally released. So long, in fact, that it actually got embarrassing for us in Topeka. Our friends had started to believe that we made the whole thing up. Finally, a UPS truck showed up at Dave's house. In the package was our album. We all gathered around the Stereo, and listened to ourselves. Suddenly, when it got to "Lonely Wind," Steve stood up and said "Who's that singing?" Someone said what we all were thinking. "You, of course, Steve." "No! I hear background voices. I didn't sing that." Sure enough, when we listened closely, they were there. Steve was pretty angry about that, and justifiably. Eventually though, the incident blew over, and was lost in the excitement over the release of our album. The guys from Kansas had arrived. At last our career was launched – and that is the miracle of our "Adventures in the Big Apple."

Guitar Miracles

Miracles. Everyone has heard of them, some of us have experienced them, perhaps even multiple times. I will enthusiastically confess that I am of the latter group. The dictionary describes a miracle as "an extraordinary event manifesting divine intervention in human affairs." For the less theologically inclined, "an extremely outstanding or unusual event, thing, or accomplishment."

Anyone would have to admit, the Parting of the Red Sea, or Christ feeding the Five Thousand are miraculous events. But how often do relatively minor miracles get overlooked because they are not so dramatic? Are we embarrassed to mention them, or do we even notice them? Sometimes we have to notice that a naturalistic explanation of an event is simply not going to work. The evidence is too overwhelming. I will give you an example, actually three, from my own life. Although there are many others I could tell you about, and they are much more dramatic, I am going to relate these three because they could so easily be explained as "just peculiar occurrences."

Guitars. Now what could possibly be miraculous about guitars? Well, I will tell you the tale of three "miraculous" guitars I have owned.

(This first segment of this story appeared in the book "Between the Strings" by John August Schroeder)

"Miracle" Number 1: (1991) In the early days of Kansas, we were touring the Southwest, where the dryness of the air around Albuquerque caused the neck of my Gibson SG to warp beyond play-ability. It got to be a really serious problem. When we got back home, the band went to "Midwestern Music," a local music store, and bought me a brand new 1969 Les Paul Deluxe "Gold Top."

I played that guitar for years, writing dozens, if not hundreds of songs on it. It was, in fact, the only guitar I played for many years. When Kansas landed their first major recording contract, a little more cash began to fill the coffers and I decided I needed a new guitar. I traded in that Les Paul for, of all things, a Hagstrom Swede. I guess I was enamored with it because it came from Sweden. It wasn't long before I began to miss that Les Paul. It didn't seem to matter what guitar I played; I always regretted getting rid of it. It's something all guitarists seem to do sooner or later. Like most guitar players, I have a long list of instruments that I wish I had never gotten rid of. I don't know why we do that, but we do.

Years went by and guitars came and went. Kansas had achieved its multi-platinum success. Still, I never forgot that Les Paul even though at that time I could have had any guitar I wanted. One day in 1991, Vicci decided to drive to Florida to visit her parents. I was home alone and it was a beautiful day, so I thought I'd get into my Piper Turbo Arrow and just fly around. We were living in Atlanta at the time, and I "got a wild hair" to fly off in a Northwesterly direction. As I continued, I got the crazy idea to fly on to Kansas and drop in unannounced on some of my old friends. I landed in Topeka, rented a car, and drove down to "Steam Music," the little music store where we all used to hang out. As I walked in the door I spied a fellow I had known for years. Joe Green, who worked there, looked at me as though he had just seen a ghost. At that very moment, he was hanging a guitar up on the wall – it was my old Les Paul. Somebody had come in that morning and traded it in. He began to tell me the story of that guitar since it left my hands, where it had gone, and who had owned it. It ended up being stolen in the Southwest somewhere, and was recovered by the police. It somehow found its way back to Kansas, and when it came into the store, he immediately recognized it. And so had I.

I had played that thing so much that I literally sweated off the gold top finish. I eventually stripped it down to bare wood. Someone had changed the pickups on it, but I didn't care. I knew that serial

16

number; there was no question that this was my guitar. Seeing it again after all those years, and ruing the day I let it go, I said to him "Don't even hang it up. Don't even tell me what you want for it. Just sell it to me here and now." I put the guitar in my plane and flew back to Atlanta. I sent it up to Ken Hoover in North Carolina, who re-fretted it got it back into shape. Now that I am the owner, it's not leaving again!

"Miracle" Number 2: (2015) I walked over to my ringing phone and picked it up. It was Bob Tolford, a friend from Atlanta. Bob would call periodically, and it was always good to hear from him. "Hi Bob, what's up?" He replied that he had just seen our documentary, "Miracles Out of Nowhere." Then, he said something puzzling. "I was wondering – do you want your guitar back?" Now I have many friends who are guitarists, but Bob was not a guitar player, so I got very curious about his question. "You know," he said, "the one you wrote *Dust in the Wind* on."

The silence on my end of the phone spoke volumes. When I came to my senses, I said "What?? You mean you have had that guitar all these years?" You could have knocked me over with a feather. I had always wondered what happened to that guitar. Not knowing what a huge hit "Dust" was going to be, I had sold the guitar years ago. It was an Aria acoustic, a mid-price model, and I didn't even remember who I had sold it to. Later, of course, I regretted that decision, and often found myself wondering where it was, and who had it. "Are you serious, Bob? Would you ship it to me?" "I'll do better than that Kerry," he replied. "I'll drive it up to you." Never was Bob so welcome in our house! The legendary *Dust in the Wind* guitar had returned home.

"Miracle" Number 3: (2016) I drove down to the little Berryton, Kansas Post Office in order to mail some CD's that had been ordered, and to pick up my mail. The clerk handed me the day's mail, among which was a letter to me from one Tony Camardo, from Chicago. I did not recognize the name. As soon as I got home, I opened his letter and began reading. At first, I thought it was just a fan letter, until he began saying that he had been to one of our shows long ago in Chicago. He said that he was the guy who had traded me an old Gibson SG for the Les Paul that I was playing at the time. Once again I got very curious.

I vaguely remembered the trade for the SG. My memory of the Les Paul, however, was crystal clear. It was (another) example of trades that I would later regret. Just the week before I received the letter, I had watched our documentary again as it played on the VH1-C channel. The scene that caught my attention was the second Don Kirshner show, in which I was playing a 1974 Tobacco Sunburst Les Paul – the very guitar mentioned in Tony's letter. Then, to my astonishment, he went on to ask me if I wanted it back! He was willing to trade it for another guitar, so I shipped him a 2000 Les Paul that I had. I thanked him profusely, and a week later I had another of my old guitars back!

So are these occurrences miracles? Are they simply instances of exceeding kindness, or are they divine interventions? Perhaps they are just extraordinary circumstances. I have my suspicions, but alas I don't know. You tell me...

Two Beebs in Japan

note: A "Beeb" is a term of endearment that Vicci and I always call each other.

In January of 1980, Kansas was informed that we were going to tour Japan. That was very exciting news, particularly since we could all bring our wives along. We had toured Europe, but never Japan. The Promoter, Udo Artists Inc., was known as a very reputable company. Our crew packed up all our equipment early, since it was to be shipped (literally) on a Chinese Freighter. When it was time for us to leave, we packed our bags and flew to Los Angeles. Our attorney, Chuck Hurewitz, met us at the Airport where we signed our wills. I remember some jokes about that being a "bad omen."

The flight was long, I mean LONG! At least 10 hours. However, there was a new development. We were booked First Class! With all the flying we had done, this was a first. In fact, we had the entire upper "floor" of the Boeing 747 to ourselves. This included sleeping quarters. Exciting! Truthfully, we were so pumped up that no one got any rest. By the time we touched down in Tokyo, I was extremely tired. In fact, I felt downright flu-ish. After checking into our Hotel, it was no problem sleeping. The next morning, feeling flu-ish had turned into the flu. As it turned out, later in the day I began to feel much better. Apparently it was just "Traveler's Fatigue." Later that day Jerry Gilleland, our stage manager, called a band meeting and dropped a bombshell. He explained that the Chinese Freighter, which had all our musical equipment on board, had been in a Typhoon. All our equipment had been packed in three "watertight" containers. He said that, despite specific instructions that they be placed in the hold, that they were instead lashed onto the deck. When the waves crashed over the ship's bow, one of the containers broke loose, went over the side and sank. The second slid across the deck and peeled open like a tin can, exposing the contents to the wind and waves. The third one survived. We sat there stunned.

This was tough news. Some cars picked us up and took us down to a warehouse, where all of the equipment had been laid out on tarps in a very orderly fashion. There were Japanese guys scurrying about with lists, and working feverishly on the instruments. Some of them appeared to be soldering circuit boards. Jerry informed me that my Guitars had been in the container that had sunk. I had lost my Black Ovation Acoustic, and my Blonde Gibson 335. Most members of the band had lost something. We would be unable to perform without our familiar instruments. I remember Robby Steinhardt walking up to his Violin case and picking his instrument up. He breathed a momentary sigh of relief, but then watched it fall apart in his hands. It had been soaked in sea water for multiple days, and turned into mush. He was nearly inconsolable. He had been playing that Violin for many years, and it was his only instrument. Then Jerry told us the "good" news. The Promoter had already been in touch with several Japanese Musical Instrument companies, told them of our predicament, and they had all agreed to help furnish us with new instruments – at no charge. Jerry had given them a list of all the things we were missing, and within 24 hours everything had been restored. If it was not exactly correct, it was replaced with a reasonable facsimile. They even gave Robby a Japanese Violin which he seemed to enjoy playing. I left Atlanta with two Guitars, and returned with seven! I think it would be safe to say, that if this scenario had happened anywhere but Japan our tour would have been sunk.

The tour included the cities of Osaka, Fukuoka, Nagoya, Kyoto, and finally, Tokyo in the famous Budokan. Overall, the tour went really well. We were received not just like celebrities, but more like deities. They really roll out the "red carpet" in Japan. I remember the hordes of screaming teenage girls, dressed in their School Uniforms, who came out to meet us in every city. Our travel was by Bus, or the "Bullet Train." We had plenty of time for tourism as well, since our shows frequently had days off in between. Vicci and I found Kyoto especially fascinating. We visited all the Buddhist temples (one of my former religions) and Shinto Shrines as well. One thing I was not ready for was the number of religious statues or images. They were everywhere. I experienced one incident regarding these images. Since we had arrived in Japan, we had been noticing these carved "Lion figures" wherever we looked. In addition, there were banners depicting Lions everywhere. I was a bit curious about them, but I never asked anyone what they meant. In fact, I had a Golden Lion that Vicci had purchased for me that I wore around my neck. I wore this in place of a Cross, thinking that no one was going to ask me what the Cross meant, but they just might ask the meaning of the Lion. To me, it signified "The Lion of Judah." Anyway, Vicci and I were walking through one of the many shopping malls when a very excited Japanese fellow came up to me. He spoke English – sort of. Now, I am not making fun of his accent, but this is the way I heard it. He kept smiling and saying "Oh! Rucky Rion! Rucky Rion!" It took me a moment before I realized that he was saying "Lucky Lion!" I should have known, since all the Japanese interviewers called me "Kelly Rivgen." I never did find out the significance of the Lion figures. It must have had something to do with the season. Obviously, it meant something important to the Japanese.

Another impression of Japan was one of extreme cleanliness. Everything seemed so clean. Even their taxicabs were spotless, with little white towels for wiping your hands, and air fresheners that smelled like fresh peaches. Also everywhere we went Vicci took note of the cute little Japanese babies. I mean, they were adorable! And the food... I recall one morning getting up and going down on the street to have a real Japanese Breakfast. The curious thing was, the menus in all the restaurants were not in English, which I didn't expect anyway. They consisted of wax models of the food that the restaurant offered in the window. You just had to point. All of the food we had in Japan was just excellent. It was not, however, what you would find at Benihana. Sometimes you didn't know exactly what you were eating unless you asked. One big surprise was the

Pastries. Man, I had no idea of the exceptional Japanese baking skills!

You sure can get in trouble with a word being mistranslated. Everyone told us, before we left, to be sure to get an authentic Japanese Massage. I was interested, and made a note of it. So when we got to Fukuoka, I called down to the front desk and ordered a Massage for two. An exceedingly polite woman showed up very shortly, carrying a stack of clean white towels. It didn't take long to find out that she didn't speak a word of English. Now, Vicci and I had both read James Clavell's "Shogun." Feeling somewhat confident that we understood a bit about Japanese culture, and armed with my "Traveler's Japanese Dictionary," we were ready for our massage. I motioned for the masseuse to begin with Vicci. This lady was all business, and got Vicci in position on the bed. I had heard that there we two different types of massage. There was the authentic kind, and a very "toned down" version for American tourists. Well, I had come all the way to Japan for this experience, and I wanted the real thing. I opened up my dictionary, and looked up the Japanese word for massage. She was just starting to go to work on Vicci, when I got her attention and said "Ama." This was the word I had looked up. She gave me a look like I had just lost my mind, and resumed on Vicci. Hmmm. I looked once again in my book and verified that I had the right word. It was correct. "Ama." I said again. This time she sat up on the bed and began speaking very rapidly (and with great gusto I might add) in Japanese. She kept gesturing with her hand, as if trying to communicate something diving or falling. Sure that I had the right word, I tried one last time. "Ama." Instantly she jumped off the bed, and began dialing the front desk on the phone. A very animated conversation followed. When she got off the phone, she picked up her towels, and began walking backwards toward the door, all while bowing repeatedly, and saying something in Japanese which sounded very, well...apologetic. She bowed once more, closed the door and she was gone. Vicci and I just stared at each other. She shrugged and said "What was that all about?" "I don't know." I answered. "I was just trying to tell her to give you an authentic massage." Our massage adventure was obviously over, so we went to bed and watched a John Wayne movie, laughing at the overdubbed voices. The next morning, still perplexed about my language difficulties, I walked up to Kink Kume, one of our translators. I told her about my troubles the night before. "Well, what were you saying to her?" she asked. "I was telling her Ama." I said. She gave me a quizzical look. "You were saying *what*?" "Ama." I said again. Kink doubled up with laughter. "What's so funny?" I asked. "You were telling her to Dive for Pearls!" she said as she giggled. Apparently, I had the right word, but I was pronouncing it all wrong, with the emphasis on the wrong syllable. Man, did I feel like a fool. The moral of this story: Speak in a language that you know, especially when ordering a massage!

Our adventure continued. We returned to Tokyo, where we had a couple of days off before we were to perform at the Budokan. Back in the States, several years before, I had signed an endorsement agreement with the Korg Musical Instruments Company. I was very enthusiastic about their polyphonic synthesizers, several of which they had given me in exchange for doing some print ads for them. They knew I was in Tokyo, and offered to take Vicci and I out to dinner. Naturally, we accepted. The owner of the company, Mr. Katoh, (Mr. Korg himself!) was to send a representative to pick us up at 7pm. Knowing that in Japan, things are very punctual, I told Vicci to make sure that we were ready and waiting in the Lobby. We got downstairs at 6:55, to make sure. 7:00 arrived, no representative. 7:01. 7:02. 7:03. Suddenly, a Japanese man burst into the room. He had obviously been running, and was clearly out of breath. He ran up to us, and started bowing repeatedly. He was apologizing profusely for his tardiness. "Don't worry about it. No harm done." I said. "In the USA, three minutes isn't very late." He ushered us into the back of a Black Limousine, and introduced himself as Mr. Hiro Yokose. His English was not perfect, but it was close. Then he introduced us to a slightly more elderly gentleman who was seated in the car. "This is Mr. Katoh." We shook hands. Mr. Yokose explained that Mr. Katoh spoke no English, so he would translate for us. Mr. Katoh looked very distinguished, if not a bit imposing. We made small talk in the Limo, and then arrived at an extremely tall building and took the elevator to the top floor. My impression of this restaurant was that it was very exclusive. The view out the windows from this "Skyscraper" was quite impressive.

The head waiter ushered us to a private dining room, and seated us around a large grill. It was just like the Japanese restaurants at home, except much fancier, and we were in a private room. The waiter brought steaming white towels for our hands. The dinner began with a couple of unidentifiable appetizers. More small talk, before it got interesting. Mr. Katoh said something to Mr. Yokose in Japanese. Mr. Yokose turned to me, and looked a bit embarrassed, or uncomfortable. He said, "Mr. Katoh wants to know, in America, do you wash hands before eating?" Now it was my turn to be uncomfortable. Mr. Katoh had been "eyeing" us all evening, as if searching out how these young Americans were going to react. Sensing what was happening, I looked Mr. Katoh directly in the eye and said, "Tell Mr. Katoh, that since I was a child, my Mother always taught us to wash hands before eating. This is common in America, but sometimes we are not able to, if perhaps we are getting a Hamburger at a drive-through window." He stared at me for a couple of seconds, and then nodded his head as if to say "Well answered." Mr. Yokose just said "Ahh..."

A team of white-coated waiters wheeled what appeared to be a large aquarium into the room. In it, were swimming the largest Prawns I had ever seen. At this sight, Vicci's eyes were riveted. Mr. Yokose said "Ah, Dancing Shrimp!" We were about to see them dance. The waiter grabbed one of the Shrimp with prongs and flung it on the hot grill, directly in front of Vicci. The giant Prawn began flopping and "dancing" about, and Vicci screamed and recoiled in horror. The Japanese men seemed quite amused at her reaction. But this was not the coup de grâce. The waiter took a spatula, and pressed down on the unfortunate invertebrate. It feebly resisted, and then gave up. Vicci nearly fainted. It was all Mr. Katoh could do to keep from laughing, which would have been impolite to his guest. Vicci recovered her composure, and she actually enjoyed the Shrimp once she got used to their visible demise. They were the best I had ever tasted, and certainly the freshest!

Mr. Katoh was not through questioning me. He waited until three of four of these big Prawns had been served, and were sitting on my plate. Again he said something to Mr. Yokose, and waited for him to translate, with the faintest hint of an impish grin on his face. Mr. Yokose looked a bit surprised when he turned to me and said "Mr. Katoh says, In Japan, real men eat the heads." All were silent, and everyone at the table was looking at me. I thought to myself, "OK, Kerry. He's challenging you. This is right out of "Shogun". There is no question, the only way out of this is that you have got to choke down one of the Shrimp heads. Otherwise, you are dishonored and not a real man." I accepted the challenge. Slowly, and very deliberately, I picked up a Shrimp, stuck its head in my mouth, and crunched it very loudly, never taking my eyes off of Mr. Katoh. We stared at each other for a few seconds, before he smiled at me for the first time. I had passed his test. From then on, I was "in" with him! The questioning, however, was apparently not over. "Mr. Katoh wants to know, how old do you think he is?" said Mr. Yokose. Again, Mr. Katoh peered at me and was awaiting my reaction. Now, this was a loaded question. If I guessed too old, I might offend him, if I guessed too young, I run the risk of appearing foolish. Before I could answer, the translator said "Mr. Katoh say "I am born again." This, I was *not* prepared for, in fact I must have appeared stunned. "Surely he is not telling me that he is a Christian?" I thought. Mr. Katoh just smiled, and began speaking for a long time, and very passionately, with Mr. Yokose. He occasionally glanced at me.

When he was finished talking, Mr. Yokose began telling me what he had said. "I am 35 years old." I looked at him, and I'm sure I could not disguise my astonishment. He was clearly much older than that. After watching me, carefully, and waiting for his statement to sink in, he resumed his story. "Near the end of World War Two, I joined the Imperial Japanese Navy. I was eighteen years old. I was trained to Pilot a secret weapon called a Kaiten. It was a suicide weapon, a manned torpedo. We knew the Americans were planning to invade our homeland. There were many Warships off our coast, and I was assigned a mission. I became Kamikaze. Since I would not be returning from my mission, my Funeral was held, I said my goodbyes, and they gave me a Death Certificate. When it came time for my mission, I prepared myself. I put on my diving gear and drove my Torpedo directly at the American ship, just as I had been trained to do. As I drew near, I braced myself, and I heard a loud CLUNK! At first, I thought I had been blown up, but I slowly realized I was alive. My Torpedo was a dud! For some reason the fuse had failed to ignite. After floating for a while in the dark, a Japanese boat picked me up and took me ashore. A few days later, Nagasaki was bombed, and the War ended. Legally, I had been declared dead, so I had to get a new Certificate of Birth. I was born again in 1945, so I am 35 years old." Now, I was truly speechless. I must have been sitting there with my mouth hanging open. I looked at Vicci just to make sure I had actually heard this story, and I was not dreaming. Her eyes confirmed it. Mr. Katoh just sat there, looking profoundly satisfied. I shook my head and said "Please tell Mr. Katoh, that is one of the best stories I have ever heard." (and it is!) We said our farewells in the back of the Limo as it dropped us off at the Hotel. Now, almost every time I play a musical note on one of my Korg instruments, I remember that evening with the "Dancing Shrimp" and Mr. Katoh. In fact, as I am writing this, I said a short prayer that perhaps he truly became Born Again.

On to another adventure. The Japanese CBS Records representatives had lined up an evening event for Kansas – a dinner of "Shabu Shabu" at one of Tokyo's finest Dining Establishments. The band and all our wives were escorted through Tokyo (in Limosines of course) and seated around a large table, Japanese style, at the Restaurant. The gentlemen from CBS were seated opposite us. As I recall, they all spoke very clear English. They told us that Shabu Shabu was one of the finest Japanese dishes to be had. The guys in Kansas, including myself, were clueless as to what it was. One of the Reps explained that it consisted of paper-thin slices of prime rib-eye steak, cooked in a nabemono, which is sort of a Japanese cooking-pot. "Dip it for just a few seconds in the hot broth, but no longer!" he said. Now that we had been instructed in the ways of Shabu Shabu, Kansas was ready to chow down. Man, this stuff was awesome, and extremely delicate. About two seconds of cooking and your mouth would just explode with "Essence of Beef!" It was truly delicious. Also excellent was their Sake. Somehow, it just tasted better than any that we had enjoyed at home.

There was, however, one very mysterious item at this dinner. It was a little white ball, roughly the size of a ping-pong ball. It resided in a small accessory bowl next to our plates. The CBS Reps made no mention of it, nor had the waiters. All the Kansas guys were eyeing the Japanese to see when, and what, they were going to do with it. We just didn't know. None of them had touched it. Meanwhile, Vicci was engaged in a vigorous conversation with the wives. They were all enjoying the dinner, and perhaps even more, the Sake. I saw Vicci's eyes fall on the little white ball. She took her chopsticks (called *hashi* in Japan) and picked it up. Suddenly the room fell silent. Every Japanese eye was fixed on Vicci. Oblivious, Vicci said "Oh, what's this little thing?" and popped it into her mouth. The CBS Reps were frozen. She began chewing. And chewing, and chewing, and chewing some more. I thought I noticed her cheeks were bulging. Yes, they definitely were bulging! She looked at me with a "Help me, what's happening to me?" look on her face. She valiantly attempted to chew the little ball, but it was very rapidly becoming a *very big ball* in her mouth. Bless her heart, her face was growing red with embarrassment. I looked at the Japanese men, desperate for some advice. Suddenly, Vicci took her napkin, and ejected the white ball into it. Now, the CBS men were laughing at her. Some had tears in their eyes.

When the laughter died down, they explained what had happened to my unfortunate wife. The little white ball was a "yeast ball." The paper-thin slices of Beef, although delicious, were not very filling. You would have to eat a truckload of them to feel full. When you were through with the Shabu Shabu, you were supposed to just pop the ball into your mouth and swallow it, without chewing it. It would then expand in your stomach, creating the sense of fullness. Ingenious – if you had been privy to that information. Vicci eventually got over her embarrassment, and now it makes us laugh.

The Budokan was originally built for the 1964 Olympics for Martial Arts competition. It would be our last gig on this tour of Japan. We were there for our afternoon sound check. I was onstage checking my Guitar when I noticed a young Japanese guy standing off to the side of the stage. He appeared to be holding a Guitar case. Whenever I glanced in his direction, he would immediately begin bowing. This happened several times before I called over one of our translators and asked him "See that guy over there? Go find out what he wants." He went up to the man and a rapid Japanese conversation ensued. More bowing. The translator came back and said "He has built a Guitar, especially for you." Always interested in a new instrument, I said "Tell him to come up on stage. I would love to see it." He opened the case to reveal one of the most interesting Guitars I had ever seen. It was custom-built, in the style of a Fender Telecaster. It had a natural wood finish, all stained red, with gold hardware. Even the fret board was red. "Wow, that's really nice." I said. "How much does he want for it?" They both gave me a perplexed stare. "He made this Guitar for you." replied the translator. "He's been working on it since hearing you were coming to Japan. It is a gift." Now it was my turn to be perplexed, or rather bowled over. I wanted to bow to him, but I knew enough of Japanese culture to know that it would be inappropriate. I told our translator that I could not possibly accept such a gift unless I gave him something in return. "Oh, no. That is not necessary." he said. "It is to me." I replied. I realized that the "gift-giving" code of etiquette is quite different in Japan than it is in the U.S., but this was my personal protocol. I called to one of our roadies and said "Get out my spare Marshall, and bring it here." I set the amp down next to the Guitar case and said "Trade?" The Guitar builder looked at the translator for approval. He gave him a nod. "Hai!" exclaimed the builder with a big smile, and broke out with prodigious bowing. So I gained another Guitar in Japan, and for sure made another friend. (I still play that Guitar, by the way.)

With the Tokyo show, our tour was finished. The next morning we said goodbye to our Japanese crew, and we were off to the airport. Though all the Guitars I had acquired went with our roadies, Vicci and I were lugging heavy suitcases packed with souvenirs. I know that we were with a band on tour, but we were still tourists. I don't remember whose idea it was, but some kind soul had figured out that Hawaii was about halfway home from Japan, and arranged for us to top off the tour with a trip to Maui. We had been there before, but we were always ready to go again. A week of sun, surf, and fresh pineapple – what a life! I doubt that Vicci and I will ever get to go back to Japan, but I am thankful that we got to go once. Those experiences were irreplaceable, if not miraculous!

Buster Keaton's Surprise

Ever since I first saw it, I knew I wanted one – a swimming pool. I *loved* swimming. My parents could not possibly afford one, so I spent my young years in the summer frolicking with garden hoses, vinyl kids' pools, farm stock tanks, ponds, and anything that would hold water. On the occasions when we were especially blessed, my Mom would drop me and my siblings off in the morning at the Gage Park or Crestview Municipal Pools for a blissful, uninterrupted day of aquatic horseplay. She would then pick us up at 5 o'clock, shivering and ravenously hungry. We were always ready to do it again the next day. When I was twelve years old, we received a special bonus to our swimming pool dreams. There was a club in Topeka, located at a local Holiday Inn called the "Buccaneer Club." It featured both an indoor and an outdoor swimming pool. My parents announced that they had enrolled us for the Summer! Hooray! Needless to say, we were deliriously happy. The daily trips to and fro began immediately.

On one of those Summer days, as my brothers and I were relishing "our" new pool, I was about to have an experience from the "Twilight Zone." It was one of those rare occasions in life that are so scarce, so extraordinary, that it is impossible to forget them. It was late in the afternoon, almost time to end another day of fun. After diving in, I swam over to the side of the pool, just for a moment of rest. I had my arms in a folded position, my head resting on them. I lifted my head, just enough to see, directly in front of my eyes – a pair of shoes. They were just inches in front of me. This was not a normal pair of footwear. They looked funny. In fact, extremely funny. They looked like old Clown shoes – from another era. I slowly raised my eyes to find out who was wearing them. My vision revealed, in succession, a baggy pair of pants, an old-fashioned style suit coat, a bow tie, and a funny looking straw hat. Initially, I did not recognize the face. Then, slowly, it emerged from my memory banks. I had seen this face before. Buster Keaton!

This was the great Buster Keaton, one of the funniest men alive, the star of the silent film era. He was just standing there, with a calm, whimsical look on his face, in front of Kerry Livgren, next to a Motel swimming pool in the State of Kansas.

I was not exactly startled, but the absolute incongruity was over-whelming. What in the world was he doing here? Had I lost my mind? I glanced around, and no one else seemed to notice him. When I looked back, he was still there. I manage to utter a nervous "Hi." He just looked at me for a long moment, waved, then turned and waddled off in his characteristic style. I just hung on to the brim of the swimming pool, stunned. Later, when Mom came to pick us up, she said "Did you have fun today, boys?" Sure did, Mom. And I saw Buster Keaton. She just gave me a quizzical look. I could see her thinking "Did he just say Buster Keaton? I'll have to ask him about that later." Eventually, we found out that he had been in town for some sort of personal appearance. He certainly appeared to me!

Shipwrecked in Hawaii

I love Maui. We were on our fourth vacation trip to the island. Ever since the first time we saw it, we were in love with the place. Vicci and I, and our infant daughter, Katy, were vacationing there along with Dave and Diana Hope. This trip was a little different. Although it was a vacation, Pastor Ricky Ryan and his wife Linda had invited Dave and I to come speak at an event sponsored by his Church, Kumulani Chapel. We had known Ricky from previous trips to the islands. Our current band, AD, was taking some time off, so we decided to spend it in Hawaii. One of our managers, Mark Ferjulian, had also flown in from L.A. to meet up with us. The speaking engagement went very well, and it was time to "recreate," which is easy to do on Maui. Ricky knew a lot of people on the island, and he arranged a sailing trip for us on a big Trimaran. He couldn't sail with us – he had to attend a Baptism that afternoon. Linda came along with us, though. The boat was owned by a friend of his named Billy, who I will simply refer to as "The Captain." Initially, Vicci was reluctant to go because of Katy, but Ricky arranged for a trustworthy babysitter from the Church, so my wife agreed to go. It was a beautiful day, as most days are on Maui. We went down to a dock in Lahaina and met the Captain and the crew. The three-hulled-boat was exceedingly handsome, with a large cabin in the center hull. We boarded it and set sail. There was a refreshing, steady breeze. Soon we could see the vista of Maui from a distance, with a beautiful rainbow over the mountains – an unforgettable sight, but we were soon to experience something else that was unforgettable.

The Captain cheerily informed us that we were going to sail North through the channel toward the East coast of Molokai, and then return. We could see the island of Lanai on our left. Lanai looks totally different than Maui. To be honest, it looks a bit bleak in comparison (but still beautiful!) As we approached Molokai, we noticed how imposing it looks. It had no beaches that we could see, on this coast anyway, and it is exceedingly mountainous. The Captain said that he would take us as close as possible, but that there were Reefs that he would have to steer clear of. We felt safe. After all, what could happen? This was Hawaii! We got close enough to see large waves breaking on the shore, and the water was an intoxicating shade of blue. All of a sudden, the boat lurched and everyone was thrown forward. There was a sickening crunching sound. The Captain immediately barked some orders to the two crewmen, and ran below to check the cabin. When he came up, I could see by the look on his face that something serious had taken place. "Everyone, Life Jackets on! Ladies, stay over here on the deck! Guys, grab these bailing buckets!" he yelled. One of the crew jumped down in the cabin, as the Captain and the other crew member put on Masks and Fins and went over the side. We started bailing. It was hard to maintain our balance, as the ship was lifted and dropped again by the surf. The center cabin was filling with water!

The Captain was apparently trying to get his boat off of the coral, but to no avail, so he climbed back aboard. We kept bailing water, but it soon became evident that we were not keeping up. We were sinking! As that thought took hold, adrenaline kicked in. "Listen up!" said the Captain. "I'm afraid you're going to have to swim to shore. There's a small beach over there. You've got to get safely beyond the coral, so you are all going to have to put on these Fins, or you will get cut, and we don't want that! Don't worry, you're going to be all right." He said not to worry. This was exciting stuff, but I don't need to tell you we were all a little worried. We all began hurriedly putting on our fins – all except Dave, who jumped over the side and promptly cut his foot on the coral. Ouch! That was going to be sore. We all started to swim towards the beach. Vicci was a good swimmer – but not good enough to be out in the Ocean with a strong current. I kept her near to me. We probably didn't have to be that concerned since we all had life preservers. Gradually we came nearer to the shoreline, while trying to stay clear of the coral. I was glad to be making progress. It was no marathon-length swim, but it seemed like it to us. What a relief it was when we finally felt the sand beneath our feet.

This was a different beach than Maui – it was a lot "wilder." We were standing, for all practical purposes, at the base of a Mountain. The slopes of Molokai rose up very sharply from where we were situated. There was all sorts of organic debris on shore. As soon as we were sure that everyone was safely ashore, a thought occurred to me. "So, what do we do now?" I started to explore our surroundings a little bit. As I walked up from the beach, I noticed that the terrain seemed more "jungle-like," in terms of the vegetation. Suddenly, I came upon a strange, and unexpected sight. Half-concealed in the underbrush was an Antique School Bus. It looked to be from the 1930's. I just stood and stared at it – it was so out-of-context. "What in the world was it doing here?" I thought. There was no road down here, that I could see. One of the rear doors was open. I stuck my head inside, and quickly realized that someone was living in it. There were a couple of T-shirts and cut-off's hanging on one of the bench seats. There was a make-shift cabinet with two cans of Red Beans. Whoever lived here, lived modestly.

Then I saw it. It almost gave me shivers. On a small wooden table rested a large book with a blue cover. It was a Urantia Book. If you have read my biography, "Seeds of Change," you can easily conceive what my thoughts were at that moment. If you have not, let me just say that Urantia was the last of the false religions that I had embraced before becoming a Christian. It would have been a rare sight anywhere – but *here*? I just stood there, my heart and my mind racing. What could I do, Lord? What *should* I do? The strangeness of this scenario was overwhelming. I still marvel at it today. I decided to do the only thing that I could do. I looked around and found a ball-point pen. I pondered whether or not the owner would be offended, but decided it was worth the risk. Opening the book to its title page, I wrote a note to its owner. My hand was quivering. I told him, in an extremely abbreviated version, what my experience with the Urantia Book had been, and how its teachings had led me down a path that was very wrong. I closed by encouraging him to find, and read, the Bible. I thought about signing the note in my name, but opted for "A Visitor." Looking around one last time, I turned and left.

I walked back down to the beach, where Vicci and the others were gathered. "Where have you been, honey?" she asked. "I'll have to tell you later. I can't talk about it yet." She gave me a very quizzical look. Linda piped up suddenly and said, while pointing, "We have to climb up there guys. There's a road up there." "Great." said Dave, while limping. His foot was starting to bother him. So we began to climb. While ascending the hill behind Vicci, I noticed her legs were extremely red. "Honey, did you have sun-block on your legs? "No." she said. "There wasn't time. I was busy bailing water out of the boat." She usually didn't get sunburned, even without sun-block, but her legs were noticeably crimson. At last we reached the road at the top, and hiked about a mile before we came to a house. Linda knocked on the door. It was answered by a man, who I can only describe as "colorful." He was a Bee Keeper. There were Hives all over the place. Linda, believe it or not, was acquainted with him. His name was Dick. She explained our "ship-wrecked refugee" situation, and asked if we could impose upon him to spend the night at his house. He and his wife graciously granted our request. He introduced his wife to us by her nickname, which was "Aome," which, he explained, meant Apple of my Eye.

We were a sorry lot of visitors. Nothing but swimming suits, and not so much as a toothbrush. Dave's coral-cut foot, and Vicci's fiery legs complicated the situation, but needless to say, we were extremely grateful for his hospitality. Vicci and I even had a private bedroom. She was very concerned about Katy, but I assured her that she would be OK. In the morning, after Coffee, Juice, and I don't recall what else, we said our goodbyes and abundant thank-you's. Linda had called Ricky as soon as we got to the Bee Keeper's house, and he had arranged for a Shuttle Flight for all of us to get back to Maui. We were not exactly dressed for travel, but what could we do? Anyway, it was Hawaii! Taxis to the small Airport on Molokai, and we were on our way home. When we landed, Maui never felt so fine. The moral of this story? Always wear fins when swimming over coral, and always wear sun-block, especially on your legs. Always prepare for the most unforeseen possible situation to arise, for it surely will. On a more Spiritual plane – I have often wondered what that individual who lived in the School Bus thought when he read my note. I wonder if he knows the awesome God who arranged, through the most extraordinary circumstances, to reach him with the truth of His Word. Miraculous!

Memories in a Whirlwind

Summer had arrived in Topeka, Kansas, June 8th, 1966. It was late afternoon, and the day was a bit humid, but as a young man of seventeen I hardly noticed. School was out, and life was good. My Band, "The Gimlets," were all at my house on Mulvane street. Scott, Tim, Dan, John, and myself were in the garage practicing, as was our frequent custom. The usual gang of neighborhood kids were gathered there as our audience. It was muggy outside, with an unsettled feeling in the air, but we were oblivious to it. It was a typical Summer day in Kansas. Suddenly my Dad walked in, and asked if a couple of us would help him to bring his Lowrey Organ home from the Eagles club in Downtown Topeka, where he had played the night before. We were almost done with practice anyway, so my friend Dan agreed to go, and we jumped in Dad's Volkswagen bus and off we went.

We loaded Dad's Organ in the bus, and on the way back home we noticed it was now *extremely* humid and still – so still that it actually felt "creepy." There was also a "greenish" tint to the atmosphere. My Dad was always hyper-sensitive to weather changes, especially since he was trained as a Pilot. He kept glancing out the windows of the bus. We were just blocks from our house when we heard the sirens going off. Their wailing was a sound I always dreaded, but also found exciting. It was a frequent occurrence in Kansas, but nothing ever came of it, at least not for us. Still, it gave me chills. Dad whipped the VW into the garage and we jumped out. The adrenaline was already pumping. My Mom stuck her head out the door and cried "The TV says it's a Tornado, just Southwest of Burnett's Mound!" Burnett's Mound is a very large hill, on the Southwest side of Topeka. The Native Americans used to say that a Twister would never hit Topeka, because it was protected by Burnett's Mound. It appeared as though that protection was over.

We all frantically ran for the basement. My Dad ordered us all to get under the pool table. (a 1912 Brunswick) My brothers and I, plus Dan and John had trouble complying with that order – we didn't all fit. Dan ended up in a bedroom closet with a clothes basket over his head. Dad was standing at the west wall, peering out through the window well. I heard a sound that I had never heard before, like the sound of a giant turbine mixed with a background of constant thunder. I climbed out from under the pool table and said "Dad, I want to see, let me see!" He said "All right, just for a second, then get back under there." I had seen plenty of pictures and films of Tornadoes, but nothing I had imagined was like what I was looking at now. It was immense – and white. But very shortly it began to get very dirty. It was sucking up everything in its path – trees, houses, cars, mud, everything. At one point, I saw an entire house fly up the side of the funnel, relatively intact, only to be reduced to a million airborne splinters.

The sound was permanently embedded in my memory. One always hears it described as "the sound of a freight train," but in fact the "giant turbine mixed with constant thunder" that I described was pretty accurate. Occasionally, I could hear something that sounded like explosions. To cap it off, this was all blended with the wailing of the Tornado sirens. The funnel was so huge, you really couldn't tell which way it was headed. It looked like it was headed straight for our house. "Get down, son, and get back under the table!" I had never seen my Father afraid of anything before, but I could tell by the sound of his voice that this was something truly dangerous – our family was in peril. I scrambled back under the pool table. Dad was still at the window. He couldn't tear himself away from this awesome and terrible sight. The city of Topeka, despite the Indian's legend, was being demolished. It became eerily dark in our basement. That "green" sky had given way to a very dim and foreboding gray. After what must have been a couple of minutes, Dad said "It looks like it's headed North of us, towards Washburn." Washburn University was indeed about twelve blocks North of our house. We didn't know it then, but later that evening we would see the wreckage of the college. As soon as Dad was sure that the

Twister's path would not hit us he said "Let's go out and see." We all vacated our shelter and ran outside to the front yard. I was absolutely transfixed. There, just to our North, was a boiling, reeling, mass of cloud, churning its way through town and vacuuming up everything in its path. Suddenly it began raining – but it wasn't rain. "Get back in the basement!" my Father yelled. The sky over us began to pour down shingles, fragments of wood, metal, chunks of asphalt, articles of clothing, papers, toys, pots and pans, everything you can imagine, both large and small. The pieces of people's lives were landing all around us. So back in the basement we went, for another two or three minutes. When the sky had given up its debris, Dad gave us the green light to emerge once again. What we saw next was a truly amazing sight. As the colossal Tornado moved off to the Northeast, the sky behind it was absolutely clear. The sun popped out as though nothing had happened. I halfway expected to see a rainbow. (Some, in fact, reported seeing one.) Gone was the oppressive humidity. The sky was beautiful, but on the ground it was something else. The Tornado had cut a path, at times more than a quarter-mile wide, from the Southeast corner of Topeka to the Northeastern border of town. Our house, less than a mile from the Twister's swath, had not been touched. However, we were about to witness the extent of the destruction. John Pribble, our drummer, lived in a nice Subdivision just East of Burnett's mound. "I've got to get home, I have to get home!" he adamantly exclaimed. In complete agreement with him, Tim, John, and I got into the car and proceeded West on 29th St. The National Guard had not yet secured the streets. As we came over the hill, we all gasped. Where the subdivision had been, was just a vast mud flat. The Tornado had actually sucked the grass out of the ground. We drove this route every day to Topeka West High School when school was in session. I knew every inch of it – but not now. There was not one familiar landmark left, just devastation. We had no idea how to find John's house, or what was left of it. We began to drive slowly, around the debris, and found John's street by dead reckoning.

I shall never forget the look on people's faces. They were just coming out of their basements. Their look of total astonishment slowly gave way to sorrow and grief. Others were praising God that they and their families had been spared. To John's immense relief, he found his house, (or just the foundation), and his parents were all right. Tim's house was barely to the North side of the destruction, just past Gage Blvd., but it was all right. There were some really strange sights to be seen. In the middle of an acre of mud on every side, stood a Grand Piano. The house where it had been was gone, but the piano was intact. Just Southeast of where John's house had been, was a modern split-level home. The surrounding dwelling places were all gone, save this one house. It was hardly damaged. But what was curious was the pillow protruding from the West wall of the house. It had somehow been sucked through a hole in the wall about the size of a grapefruit. The next day I saw a picture of an airplane propeller stuck upright in someone's yard. Weird stuff. We found out later that we had experienced a very close call. (as if being in a Tornado was not close enough!) The Tornado's path took it right through downtown Topeka. There was a small bowling alley, the Pla-Land, very near to the Eagles club where we had been earlier. The owner was killed there, while taking shelter under a pool table. If we had lingered there a bit longer, we would have been directly in the Tornado's path. Or, if it had veered only a few blocks South, it would have hit our home, and perhaps our pool table. Thank God for His mercy.

In the weeks and months that followed, many more "Tornado Stories" would be told. The Fujita scale, the "F" designation, was not in use at the time. Applied retroactively, this Tornado was an F5, at the height of the scale. Now, many years later, it has made me a bit of a "weather freak." Every spring I prepare a "weather survival kit," and each time I hear the sirens go off, I grab Vicci and the kids, and run for that old pool table in the basement!

We Go for a Ride

One Summer day, my Dad called me and my two little brothers, Chris and Cal, and said "Hey, kids! Why don't we go for a ride!" He sounded so excited, that we immediately got excited as well. "Mom's going to go too." he stated. "All the better!" we thought. We all piled into our family car, a big gray Nash Ambassador. We backed out of our driveway, and headed for adventure and parts unknown. "Where are we going, Dad?" I asked. "Oh, nowhere in particular, we're just going for a ride." he said. His answer satisfied us, for a while, anyway. He headed out of our subdivision, then turned North on Washburn Avenue. The route was familiar, as this was the way we would go to our Aunt Lily's house. "Are we going to Aunt Lily's?" I asked. "No son, we are just driving." Dad said. Mom turned and looked at the three of us in the back seat. Her face betrayed no emotion.

Something was wrong. The tone of Dad's voice was different. I couldn't put my finger on it. He sounded very compliant and he answered our questions, but there was an almost sympathetic tone to it, as if he regretted something that was going to happen. Something was fishy. This was a curious situation. Our curiosity got the best of us, and eventually we became obsessed with our destination. We asked again, and again we got the same answer. Now it was downright suspicious – and very unlike our parents, who had always been totally honest with us. "All right boys," Mom said. "I'll tell you, it's a surprise." Chris and Cal let out a squeal. I was more reticent. There was something suspicious about the way she said it. The "surprise" announcement worked for a while, but the impatience of little kids won out. We wanted to know what the "surprise" was. Dad turned the car off of 17th St., near the University. We were going North on College Avenue – a residential neighborhood. We were in a strange place. I demanded an explanation. "Come on, Mom, tell us where we're going." She glanced at Dad, and he at her. Then she looked at me and said, "Well, kids, the truth is we are going to get your Polio Shots."

Instantaneously, both the rear doors of the Nash flew open. We were going at least 25 miles per hour. Chris and Cal shot out the right side of the car, I bailed out on the left. We hit the pavement running for our lives. The last thing I remember hearing was the screech of the tires as Dad hit the brakes, and my parents frantically yelling. I ran through yards, leaping over bushes, until I found refuge under someone's porch. I knew not the fate of my two brothers. All I knew was, I am NOT getting a shot. This was my worst fear – above all others. Ever since the first vaccination I had received at our family Doctor's office, it became a thing of dread. I HATED shots – the smell of cold alcohol, the long gleaming needle, and the smiling nurses. NO WAY!

Well, my parents managed to round us all up. After apologizing for having deceived us, they explained it was because they loved us so much that we had to get Polio Shots. They didn't want us to suffer. After they got us calmed down, we got our shots. It was a small price to pay for such love. And I never got Polio.

Inauguration Into the Big Time

The first Kansas album was out and selling reasonably well when Don Kirshner decided the band needed some exposure to the "Powers That Be" in Los Angeles. CBS Records was hosting a big party at a place (as best I can remember) called "The Bistro." There were to be lots of famous artists there, both new and established, in addition to Producers, Radio and Record Exec's, and whoever else might tag along. The obvious idea was to get everyone acquainted with each other. When I told Vicci the band was going to L.A. for a Cocktail Party, she let me know, in terms that I could not fail to understand, that she was going with me. (I would never hear the end of it if I didn't take her!)

They flew us all to Los Angeles, and we checked into a nice Hotel. When it came time to get ready for the big bash, Vicci got all "dolled up" in a beautiful and very fashionable outfit, featuring long, flowing, silky trousers. Wow! Her dark hair and "Cleopatra" eyes just knocked me out. (they still do.) I was proud to show off my lovely Georgia wife – the equal, if not superior, to anything Hollywood could produce. We went down to the lobby, and to our surprise, there were two big limousines there to transport us to the big festive affair. Whoopee! Now remember – we, being a bunch of Kansas boys, were not used to such "goings-on." We had no idea of the appropriate dress for such an occasion. Even if we did know, we certainly didn't have any of that sort of clothing in our possession. I put on one of my best T-Shirts. Rich and Dave wore their customary Overalls. Only Vicci was properly attired, bless her heart.

We gleefully piled into the Limos and began making our way to our destination. Our excitement was palpable. In a few minutes we were there. We exited the Limousines, and found ourselves standing in a crowd of people, most of whom were supposed to be there. The rest were fans and curious onlookers.

Since virtually nobody knew who we were, the fans were obviously not ours, but our arrival in the Limos insured that we were "somebody." We were escorted into the building, appropriately decorated with brass urns and ferns, and directed to a long staircase. The Doorman smiled, and told us to go upstairs to the party. The room upstairs was crowded, and filled with smiling faces and animated conversation. We didn't know anybody. Kansas drew on each other in situations like this. We had an internal sense of security among ourselves which we knew would get us through it. Besides, I thought, this could be fun! Vicci was not so confident as she drew close by my side. There were many "fashionable" ladies present. Our manager told us to just "circulate."

Almost immediately, I perceived a familiar face. It was a face I knew, not from personal knowledge, but from one of my many album covers. It was Carlos Santana. He glanced at me, a gaping fan, then resumed the conversation he was engaged in. A bit embarrassed, I turned the other way, only to find myself facing some of the members of Chicago. I was too dumb-struck to speak. This was a "Wonderland" and I had been dropped in the middle of it. What was even more amazing, was that our band was now on (nearly) equal footing with many of the musicians we idolized. Who could have imagined? We didn't exactly know what to do, or who to talk to. As the members of our band dispersed about the room, Vicci and I gravitated to the nearest wall, which we thought would provide some protection. I found myself standing next to Flo and Eddie. (of Turtles, and Frank Zappa fame.) They said something like "Some party, isn't it?" I said "Yeah, everybody's here." Then I introduced myself as a member of Kansas, and attempted to justify our attendance by making some remark about being affiliated with Don Kirshner. That drew a blank, but understanding look. Then they began joking and made some light-hearted remarks that made me feel a bit more comfortable. Actually, they were quite funny. Meanwhile, I turned around and Vicci was engaged in a conversation with a man standing in the corner. It was Roger McGuinn of the Byrds. He had noticed that Vicci was looking very uncomfortable, and had introduced himself and talked to her to made her feel more at ease. What a gentleman he was! I will always remember him for that. Feeling a bit more confident, we wandered across the room and began to chat with some very elegant looking Black ladies. We shortly found out that they were the Pointer Sisters, who would eventually make the hit song "Neutron Dance." They were a pleasure to talk to, and just as amazed to be there as we were.

Then our CBS representative decided he wanted to introduce us to a new up-and-coming band they had just signed that were from Hawaii. I didn't take note of the name of their band, but they were four very large Hawaiian guys. We shook hands, and then Vicci, always wanting to be charming, held out her hand and said "Oh, you're from Hawaii! I love Hawaii! Welcome to America!" Needless to say, they were not amused. I quickly pulled Vicci away. As I did so, she realized what she had said, and wished for all the world that she had not opened her mouth! I still never found out the name of that band...

Meanwhile, Rich and Dave were parked in front of the Buffet. Nothing will attract a member of Kansas like fresh boiled shrimp. This place had provided the biggest, best shrimp we had ever seen. The two Kansans had decimated them, and were resting from their feast at a table, while noticing all the California blonde ladies who paraded by. This was during the time of the "Farah Fawcett hairdo" that was so immensely popular. Nearly every young female had it. Dave Hope always had a snide remark handy. As one of those young damsels walked by, Dave very sarcastically called out "Hey Farah!" She whirled around. It was Farah Fawcett. "Yes?" she said. Dave's mouth hung open. Awestruck silence. She walked away. I will never forget the look on Dave's face. That was about the only time I saw someone get the best of Dave Hope.

After over-dosing on meeting various celebrities, it was time for us to leave. With Vicci on my arm, we walked to the big staircase to begin our descent back into reality. As she took the first step, she caught her foot in the long silky trousers she was wearing. The next moment happened in slow motion. I desperately tried to hang on to her, but she was slipping out of my grasp. Before I could re-act, she was sliding down the stairs. She slid all the way to the bot-tom and landed in a heap, with her pants up her legs in a very ex-posed condition. I hustled downstairs as fast as I could, and said "Honey, are you all right? She looked up, but she didn't see me – she was looking at two men standing there. She had landed right at their feet. It was Tom Jones, and Engelbert Humperdinck. They just stared. There she was, in the most vulnerable condition, lying at the feet of two of the era's most notable "heart-throbs." Tom Jones said, in his rich Welsh accent, "Ma'am, are you all right? Do you require some assistance?" Vicci quickly arranged her attire, with as much dignity as she could summon, and said "No, I'm all right, thank you." Thank God she was. I helped her to her feet. Jones and Humperdinck were acting like Gentlemen, but I am quite sure they got a laugh out of it when they were out of earshot. All these years later, so do we!

Brother Cal and the Escalator

Every so often we would go to Missouri to visit my Grandpa Mac and Ina. When I was a kid, I thought everybody had three Grandpa's like I did. We had Grandpa Charlie and Grandma Tilly (My Dad's parents who came from Sweden), Grandpa Jewell and Mammy (My Mom's Stepfather and Mother), and then there were Grandpa Mac and Ina (My Mother's Father and Stepmother.) I never asked why we had three, it was just accepted. We loved them all equally.

Years later, when I got curious, my Mom explained to me that Grandpa Mac and Mammy were once married, but they got divorced. She never said any more about it. Although divorce is rarely a good thing, the Lord took a bad thing and turned it into a blessing. I got three Grandparents out of it. Grandpa Mac lived in Appleton City, Missouri. (He always pronounced it Missour-uh.) He was a tall, soft-spoken man. He was bald, but somehow didn't look it. I heard a story that in his younger days, he used to ride the Missouri streets on his Henderson Motorcycle with a gang of his buddies. Somehow, I could never quite picture that. He ran a small Cafe, which was always a favorite with the locals. He was famous for his Fried Brain Sandwiches (Pig brains - we never even tried them), and Ina made the best Beef and Noodles on the face of the Earth.

We usually drove our family car to get there, but my Dad couldn't get off work at Goodyear to come with us, so my Mom booked us on a Greyhound Bus. We were tremendously enthusiastic about this – it was something new and different! Mom, however, would have her hands full. Watching over me and my two little brothers, Chris and Cal, was always a daunting task. We got up early in the morning when it was still dark, and my Dad dropped us off at the Greyhound Bus Depot in Topeka. Mom had us all packed in a single suitcase. We never needed much at Grandpa Mac's. When it was just getting light outside, the Bus Driver yelled "All aboard for Kansas City!" We were first in line. We picked our seats, and got settled in for this adventure. Mom sat right behind us. I can still remember the sights, sounds, and smells of that first Bus ride. Kansas City was just an hour away, but to a kid it felt like 500 miles.

We arrived at the Kansas City Bus Station, and pulled to a stop next to some other Buses. They had exotic destinations written above their windshields like "Denver" and "St. Louis." Full of adrenaline, we jumped out of the Bus and ran into the Depot. There were snacks there, and racks of postcards, and people bustling back and forth. Then, we saw it – an Escalator. "Mom, what *is* that?" (Growing up in Topeka, we had never seen one.) "It's called an Escalator. It's sort of an automatic staircase." "Oh, Mom, can we ride on it?" I asked excitedly. Chris and Cal were jumping up and down. "Yes, but be careful!" she said. Mom explained to us that she would be watching us from the Snack Bar, where she would be enjoying a cup of Coffee. I was to be in charge of Chris and Cal. We walked up to the Escalator, our eyes wide with wonder. For a while, we observed people getting on and off, before we decided to take the plunge. "OK, I'm going first." I said cautiously. I stepped on, and felt the sensation of movement as it jerked me forward. The next thing I knew, I was rising upward! When I got to the top, I immediately exited and got on the "down" Escalator. My brothers were smiling eagerly as they waited for me to get off. Now an experienced rider, I escorted them on their first Escalator ride. They were both filled with glee. We spent the next few minutes riding up and down. The adult riders just had to excuse the three young boys who had commandeered the Escalator. We graduated from just riding up and down, to running up the "down" Escalator, and running down the one that was going up. Such fun.

A word about my littlest brother, Cal. Unlike me and Chris, he was constantly getting hurt. He seemed always to have stitches somewhere on his body, and he was the "King of Scabs." If one of us got in trouble, it was usually Cal. At four years old, he was already a veteran. Cal decided he was going to try something new. He got

48

on the up Escalator, then turned and sat down on the step. Chris and I waited a couple of seconds, then stepped on behind him, standing upright. There were a couple of adults who were riding behind us. All was going blissfully well, as we rode upward. Cal was smiling. Suddenly, out of nowhere, Cal let out the most blood-curdling shriek I had ever heard. At the same instant, the Escalator ground to a halt, causing everyone riding to lurch forward. Brother Cal was wailing. I had no idea what had happened. He just sat there, at the top of the Escalator, and was yelling hysterically. I went up to him, but he was shrieking like a wild man. Apparently, he was unable to get up. I bent over him to see what was holding him. I froze. The Escalator had eaten my little brother. I had never noticed before, but there were grooves in the steps, and metal "teeth" where the steps disappeared. Those "teeth" had grabbed hold of Cal's little butt. His pants had been sucked inside, and the Escalator had him by the skin. "MOM, MOM!" I cried frantically. Cal was still howling. A crowd was starting to gather. Some of the ladies were saying things like "Oh, the poor dear" while others were snickering.

My Mother must have heard Cal's initial wail, and recognizing her son's voice, she ran up the stairs. She appeared at the top, about the same time as the Bus Depot's Custodian. The Custodian took one look and said "I know what to do." He ran off somewhere. Mom was trying to comfort Cal, who was still squalling. Suddenly, the Escalator jerked, and backed up about an inch. Cal shot up into mom's arms, whimpering, and she hurried him off to the Women's Restroom. Chris and I waited until they came out. "He's going to be OK.' Mom said. A Nurse looked him over. He just got pinched, and he's pretty humiliated." "Pinched?" I thought. That was the worst pinch I ever saw. I couldn't believe that my little brother's butt had stopped that Escalator cold.

The rest of the trip to Grandpa Mac's was uneventful compared to that. As a matter of fact, most of the many trips I have taken over the years have been uneventful compared to that!

Encouragement Out of Nowhere

I was hard at work on my first solo album, "Seed of Change." After achieving two hit albums with Kansas, our manager, Budd Carr, had negotiated solo deals with CBS Records for both Steve and myself. This was new territory. It was exciting and liberating, being on my own, but the album was taking a toll on me. The problem was not the music. Several of the songs I had already written, thinking that they would perhaps be on a future Kansas album, but I set them aside because they were either stylistically or lyrically inappropriate for the band. I had plenty of compositions. Nor was it the fact that I had to secure the scheduling for all the various musicians and singers, which was something I never had to do with Kansas. It was something else.

I was a new Christian. I had just become a believer the previous year, and I was excited to reflect my newly found faith in my lyrics. In a sense, this was nothing new. Many, if not most of the songs I had written in the past were expressions of spiritual longing, or searching. There was a lot of weight on my shoulders, and part of the "fatigue" that I was feeling was spiritual in nature. I knew enough of the Bible to know that being a Christian meant "going against the grain" of the World. I was already experiencing some issues with my fellow band members. There was an unspoken tension, or uneasiness, when Kansas was together. Comfort was to come from another, and unexpected, source.

One day, when I was in the Control Room, the Studio Secretary stuck her head in the door and said "Kerry, you have a phone call." "It's got to be Vicci," I said to Brad Aaron, the engineer. I knew it was her, since she was the only person that knew I was there. It couldn't be anyone else, since she was the only one to whom I had given the phone number. I walked down the hall to where the phone was, and picked it up. "Hello?" It was a man's voice that answered, a voice I did not recognize. "Is this Kerry Livgren?" "Yes it is," I answered. "Who am I speaking to?" I said. (Unfortunately, for reasons that the reader may come to understand, I cannot recall his name.) He said "My name is so-and-so. I am a businessman, and I am a Christian." His voice sounded very nervous, or perhaps frightened. "I 'm standing here in the Atlanta Airport, between flights. I really don't want to bother you, but I have something to tell you." Intrigued, I said "OK, I'm listening."

The businessman continued. "OK, you're going to think I'm nuts." he said. "I probably would if I received this phone call from a stranger. I've never had anything like this happen to me before, but as I was walking through the Airport, I suddenly heard a voice. It said, very clearly, 'Call Kerry Livgren at Axis Studio, and just tell him to be encouraged.' I couldn't tell if I had heard an auditory voice, or if it was in my mind, but I looked up the number to the studio and called. There was no doubt what this voice told me to do, so that's what I'm doing now. Be encouraged." A 'goose-bumpy' feeling came over me. I could not get past the thought that no one but Vicci knew where I was, and she certainly would not tell a total stranger.

Now it was my voice which got quivery. "Well," I said. "I have never received a phone call quite like this before, either. I would have to admit, it's quite encouraging." We chatted for another minute or two, both of us marveling at what had happened, then we said goodbye and hung up. As I walked back down the hallway to the Control Room I was smiling, and my eyes were brimming with tears – two seemingly incompatible reactions. The thought that the Lord cared enough about one lone Musician to arrange something like this, a near miracle, was overwhelming to me. Brad looked at my face when I walked in and said, "What's wrong?" "Absolutely nothing!" I replied.

Ambushed from Behind

"The Gimlets" were my first band. Our great claim to fame, such as it is, was a series of Television appearances we made on KFEQ TV in St. Joseph, Missouri. The show, called "Let's Dance," was hosted by a DJ named Bill Foster. He also had a little business "on the side," as a Promoter. He would set up gigs all over Northwestern Missouri, in every little town you could imagine. We would play, always for a percentage of the door, in local American Legion Halls, Moose Lodges, Grange Halls, etc., or any empty building he could procure. Though we were teenagers, and too young to be completely legal, he booked us into a few Beer Bars as well. For a while, he kept the Gimlets alive.

"Let's Dance" was a live TV show in which a (hopefully) decent local Band would appear, and play for half an hour (between commercials.) A large teenage audience was there to dance. We could pick up KFEQ in Topeka, so we had seen the show a couple of times. I don't know how Bill Foster had heard of us, seeing as how we were from Kansas. It is quite possible that my Mother was involved in getting us on the show. She sometimes acted as our manager, (and devoted fan), in those early days. So we got a phone call from Bill, offering us a date for The Gimlets to appear. Needless to say, we joyously accepted. We immediately held a band practice in my basement, and another, and another, until we were reasonably confident that we could do a seamless show. Our song list featured "show stoppers" like "Come on Down to My Boat," "Bald Headed Woman," and "Woolly Bully." We even did a couple of my original songs, which was unheard of from a High School-aged band. They were titled "What's the Difference?" and "World of Lies." We were proud to debut them on Television!

We did our first appearance on "Let's Dance" at the TV Studio. To us, this was a place full of wonders, if not a little intimidating. It was full of cables, electronic equipment, and large Television Cameras. Very imposing. When everyone was ready, Bill Foster came out and told the audience and the band what to expect. Then the red "On the Air" light came on, and with his best "DJ" voice he said something like "Welcome to Let's Dance! Today, all the way from Topeka, Kansas, we have The Gimlets!" Then he waved to us and we launched into our opening number. Once we got started, it was almost just another gig – almost. Except for the fact that we were uncharacteristically nervous, and the irritating interruptions to "hear from our sponsors," it was a High School dance. The move-ment of the Camera operators was a constant reminder, however, that we were playing live on Television.

Before we knew it, it was over. The audience was filing out, and stagehands were coiling up cables. Bill came up to us and said "Very nice job, guys. Way to go! You looked and sounded great. I'd like to book you some other gigs, and, I'd love to have you back on the show." This is where all those aforementioned performances in Northwestern Missouri came from. We played for him in towns like Gallatin, Trenton, Platte City, and many others. We were trav-elers! Just give us my Dad's '61 Plymouth and a trailer and we were good. As far as having us return to an appearance on TV – man, did he deliver! We got a call from him a couple of months later about doing a special "Let's Dance" show at the new Mall which they had built in St. Jo. This was quite a gig! We set up on a large stage in the middle of the Mall. There was a big crowd gath-ered, in front, on the sides, and even behind the band. Bill "coached' this crowd on the fine points of a live Television appear-ance. We knew the drill. Unfortunately, we found ourselves in a sit-uation with a bunch of "hecklers" behind us. There was about half a dozen of these punks. They were calling us every name in the book and throwing spit-wads and such at us while we were live on the air. When the first commercial break came, we tried to get Bill's attention – to no avail. When we started playing again, it got worse. Tim, Scott, Dan, and I had some cover, as we were all standing in front of our amplifiers. Not so for Carl Corona, our drummer. He was an easy target for them. I turned and looked at him, and he had a look of "near panic" on his face.

The heckling got worse. They were determined to make fools of The Gimlets and disrupt our performance "live on the air." Carl was doing his best to ignore them and play his drums, but it was impossible. Then, during a commercial, one of the hecklers got a bright idea. I have no idea where he found a box of paper clips and a big rubber band. Perhaps he came equipped with them. When we began to play again, he opened fire. He was bending the clips open, and firing them at us with the rubber band. It was a formidable, and potentially dangerous weapon. One of these little silver "arrows" whizzed just past my ear. I moved forward as much as I could, while still attempting to sing in the microphone. Carl was not so lucky. The guy drew the rubber band as far as it would stretch, and launched one his projectiles. It flew at Mach 2, and hit the back of Carl's head with a pronounced "THOK." The whole bunch of hecklers all looked at each other, and ran off in different directions. Meanwhile, we were still on TV. I had never prayed for a commercial before, but I think I did then. When it came, we immediately checked out Carl's "paper clip" wound. I tried to gently to remove it, but it was embedded in his skull! Eventually, of course, it came out, and Carl was none the worse off. I was not to play live on TV again until 1974 – the first appearance by Kansas on the "Don Kirshner's Rock Concert" program. Rest assured – I was looking over my shoulder for hecklers!

Kansas and the Doors

In the summer of 1970 the first rendition of the band known as "Kansas" got an opportunity to go to New Orleans and play for a couple of weeks at a club in the French Quarter called the "Inner Section." The reason we got this job was that Ehart, Hope, and Williams had been down in Louisiana before as members of "White Clover," and had played a few of the local Clubs and Concert Halls. As well as performing, they had become acquainted with Don Fox, the owner of the infamous "Warehouse." The Warehouse hosted a lot of well known recording acts. Fox later became a very influential promoter, and years later he would promote several of the big Kansas tours.

We were quite excited about this trip. (Any road trip was exciting for us!) One of the reasons I was particularly enthused was that there were quite a few musicians in New Orleans that I would probably never get a chance to meet while living in the State of Kansas. On one occasion, Jim Morrison of the Doors came in to the club where White Clover was playing and got up on stage and "jammed" with them. Actually, I think the "jam" consisted of reciting some ad lib free form poetry, and singing. Being a big Doors fan, I found this story intriguing. The Kansas band was so dirt poor that at one point we wrote Morrison a letter begging him for money to keep us going. (Understandably, we never heard back.)

The "Inner Section" was a small club on Royal Street, as I recall. We could barely fit on the stage, and we had to play several sets every night. Being a "financially challenged" rock and roll band as we were, we stayed with a friend and former manager of the band, Phil Musso. He had a small house down at the end of St. Charles Street near the Camellia Grill. We used to ride the Trolley to the Quarter to hang around all day before we had to play. On nights when we weren't playing we would go over to the Warehouse and see whoever was there. I got to see "The Band," which was quite a treat as I was a big fan of theirs also. I always thought Garth Hudson was one of the most unique Keyboard players I had ever heard. While we were there we saw a poster for the Doors who were coming the following week. We went nuts and begged Fox to let us open the show for them. He always liked us, so he set it up with the Doors management and they gave us the gig. (In those days things like that happened!)

We thought we had our big break. Needless to say, the anticipation and excitement were at an all time high. Just to be able to play at the Warehouse would have been a big deal, but to open for the Doors was premium! We showed up early to set up for the show. Kansas, with six members, was a huge band, and I remember being amazed at how "Spartan" the Doors equipment was. We kept looking around and wondering when they would show up. The Warehouse had but one small dressing room, which both bands had to share. With today's prima donna band attitudes, that would be unheard of. It was a small room above the stage with a low ceiling and big wooden beams overhead. Kansas barely fit in there, much less anyone else.

At last the Doors came walking in – all except Jim Morrison. We must have been pretty "starry-eyed." I felt like I was in the presence of some sort of deities. I remember having a conversation with Ray Manzarek about the keyboards he used. I asked him why he never used anything else other than his Vox organ, like a Mellotron. (I was enamored with those things.) He told me the Doors just didn't need anything else for their sound, and of course he was right. Though we were in a reverie, we kept wondering when Morrison would show up. At last he appeared at the Door, no pun intended. Phil Ehart, who had met him before, stood up and said "Guys, this is Jim Morrison." I timidly stepped forward and shook his hand, but Dan Wright, our organist, jumped up from the chair he was in, struck his head on one of those low wooden beams, and was knocked out cold on the floor. Morrison just looked down at him expressionless. I remember thinking "Oh Boy, not only is this profoundly embarrassing, but now Dan is out and we can't play without him." Fortunately he came to, and was able to play.

Jim Morrison definitely had an unusual presence. There was an air of unpredictability about him. We could hardly take our eyes off of him. At one point, he looked up at the wooden beam, hoisted himself up, and hung upside down from it like a bat. He then started to recite some of his (ad lib) poetry. We were transfixed. I couldn't believe I was in the room witnessing this. Then he suddenly dropped off the beam and landed on the floor, laying there as if dead. The other members of the Doors seemed not the least concerned – as if this happened every day. Morrison got up, brushed himself off, and acted as if nothing unusual had happened. I don't recall a single word of the poem he recited.

I don't think Kansas had one of our better performances that night. Things never seem to go well when there is that much adrenaline flowing. I remember thinking that everything sounded out of tune, and it felt as if I had tape around my fingers. After our set, I went out into the audience to watch the Doors. That band created an atmosphere that was like no other. There was something very dark and mysterious about their music. I don't believe I have seen a singer, before or since, that had such command over an audience. When they were playing "When the Music's Over," and they came to the part of the song where Morrison sings "we want the world and we want it...," he paused, the band went completely silent, and he slowly unscrewed his mic stand from its base and held it like a spear. You could have heard a pin drop in that place. Nobody breathed. I remember thinking "is he going to throw it?" NOWWW!!! Fortunately he did not, but it was quite an electric moment. There was more. When it came to "Light My Fire" the Doors waved us up on to the stage to play with them. Our Sax player, Larry Baker, and our Flutist, Don Montre, got to do most of the playing, but it was quite a thrill indeed.

It was several years later before Kansas became a major recording artist in our own right, but I will never forget that evening. What perhaps makes it even more memorable is that their New Orleans concert, as I understand it, was the last performance Jim Morrison ever did with the Doors. After that he went to France and never returned.

An Unplanned Adventure

It was one of those Georgia mornings when the Sunshine was so bright and the sky was so blue that it almost felt unreal. It was December 29th, 1981. Vicci had driven down to Daytona after Christmas to visit her parents. I don't recall exactly why I had remained at home, but it was of no concern since we had planned on my flying down to be with them later. Well, "later" was this beautiful morning, and I had my brand new Cessna 172 waiting for me at the airport. I was always eager for any opportunity to fly it, and this day would prove to be an airborne adventure. I called and got a Weather Briefing, and, as expected, it was forecast to be clear all the way to Ormond Beach, which was the nearest airport to where Vicci's folks lived.

I packed my duffel bag and the necessary Sectional Charts, and drove to my home airport, McCollum Field on the Northwest side of Atlanta. I checked my fuel, conducted my Pre-flight, and executed a flawless takeoff. (if I say so myself – Pilots are always so proud!) McCollum is an uncontrolled field, so I tuned my radio to the local Unicom frequency just to be safe. After all, this is crowded Atlanta airspace. I was very much looking forward to this 365 mile flight. After successfully circumventing Atlanta, I was at altitude and headed South for Florida. I had flown this route before, but I set my VOR radio to Macon just to make sure it was working. I planned to set it on Ormond Beach as I came within range. When I reached Waycross, I checked the Weather on their frequency and it was still clear all the way. In fact, out my window the view was still pretty spectacular. As I drew nearer to Jacksonville, I could see the coast to my left. To my front was an almost infinite view of Florida ahead, and Georgia behind. In what seemed like an instant, I noticed a strange sheen to my left over the ocean. As I progressed southward, it slowly became recognizable as some sort of low-hanging cloud front, or fog bank. "Wow, that's interesting" I thought to myself. This certainly was not part of the forecast. Just to be certain, I radioed Jacksonville, and they confirmed that it was indeed a fog bank, and it was moving inland. I asked them about Daytona-Ormond, and they said it was still clear.

Here is where I made my first mistake. Perhaps it was understandable, but still it was an error in judgment. I had only logged about 150 hours in my logbook at that point – still a very young pilot, and I had not experienced any sort of life-threatening Weather scenarios. To be sure, my training taught me what I probably should have done. Turn around, and fly back to clear weather, or land somewhere nearby and wait it out. Instead, looking ahead at the clear sky, I opted to try and make Ormond Beach Airport. That fog could not possibly make it that far inland, or so I thought. Perhaps I had a bit of the "disease" most Pilots fall ill to "I can make it-itis." No one likes to admit failure. The consequences of my pride, however, would nearly cost me my life.

I flew on. I could clearly see it now – a thick, gray, blanket moving rapidly to the West. My sense of unease was becoming a sense of alarm. I was now only 40 miles from my destination, but I decided to abort, and turn back. I banked the aircraft to reverse my course and head back to Waycross to land. When I saw what I faced, my alarm was real. Turning around was no longer an option. The fog now extended as far as I could see, in front and behind. I no longer had enough fuel to go anywhere but Ormond. I began rehearsing in my mind the procedure to make such a landing – the kind I had only read about. I turned back around, heading South. I knew that there was a VOR on the field at Ormond that would give me a heading to the Airport. I was not an Instrument rated Pilot, so I knew that all I could do was locate the Airport, but I would be "flying by the seat of my pants" as far as making an approach. It was at this point that I first felt fear. It was welling up within me. Fear of crashing my airplane, fear of losing my young family, fear of losing my life. I instinctively knew that, if I gave in to it, and it became panic, that I was a "goner." I suppressed it. I would need to have all my attention devoted to my piloting.

Here is where I made my second mistake. I could have, and probably should have, got on the radio and declared an emergency. Then someone could have "talked me through it" and got me on the ground. But that thought never occurred to me. I was so focused on flying the airplane, and pushing back my fear, that I didn't think to do it. Now I have to make an approach to landing. I knew that I was somewhere over the airport, but I couldn't see it. I circled several times trying to decide what to do. I remembered an occasion during my training when I asked my instructor what to do if you were experiencing an engine failure at night. He looked at me and said "Well, you turn on your landing light. If you don't like what you see, just turn it off." I laughed when he said that, but this was no joke. There are a lot of tall Pine trees in this part of Florida. Lord, don't let me hit one of those. I knew that Florida was only a few feet above Sea Level, so I set my altimeter so I would know just before I hit the ground. I chose a compass heading for the runway, and began my descent. I sunk into the dark gray opaqueness, which grew darker by the second. I lowered flaps and slowed my airspeed to just above a stall. It's strange – all sorts of scenes from my life were passing before my eyes. I opened my window and stuck my head out to see if I could see anything below me. I couldn't even see my own landing gear! It grew darker. My altimeter indicated I was only 100ft above the ground.

At least I remembered to do one thing that they didn't mention in my Pilot training. Pray. I was praying like I have never prayed before. I did not have time to pray with an abundance of words, but with an earnestness of thought – O' Lord, save me! The moment had come. A strange awareness entered my mind – so this is how I die. I suppressed that also. The altimeter was nearing zero. Lord, please don't let me harm anyone else on the ground. I gently flared the airplane and braced myself for the impact – and eternity. Then, I heard the last sound I expected. It was the familiar "squeak" of tires on the runway, followed by the nose-down attitude of the aircraft, followed by the sound of the aircraft rolling on asphalt. I still could not see clearly what was happening – the fog was all the way to the ground. The other thing that was "fogged in" was my mind. I didn't know if I was still alive, dreaming, or dead. Instinct took over. I pressed on the brake pedals and felt the plane come to a stop. I turned the key off. Silence. I sat there for a couple of minutes, stunned. Slowly the realization came – I was alive, I had landed, and the Lord had delivered me. Then I heard someone shouting. A dark figure emerged from the haze "This airport is closed! How did you get in here?" I don't remember exactly what I said to him, but it was something like "I don't know." Then the shakes began – I sat there just quaking in my seat for several minutes. Eventually, I climbed out, got the aircraft safely tied down and made a phone call to my Father-in-law who came and picked me up. Good thing – I don't think I could have driven a car at that point.

As the years have passed, the recollection of this event has not faded for me. How could it? The odds that I was perfectly lined up with that runway, with visibility zero, are astronomical. Only the Lord could have arranged that.

The Cows Got Out

We had moved to the country in 1985. I described many of my "Farm Adventures" in the last edition of "Seeds of Change," but here is one story I left out of that book. It is a tale of appalling ignorance on my part, but here goes.

We were living on 55 acres of beautiful Georgia land. It had satisfied my longing for rural life, but I was ready to get serious and transition into the "big time." Though I now owned a Ford Tractor, a 4-wheel drive Dodge, and a shiny new Kawasaki ATV, I would never be a real Farmer until we got some cows. The problem was that the sum total of my agricultural knowledge was near zero. I was a living example of the character "Oliver Douglas" in the TV series "Green Acres." Vicci fulfilled the role of his wife, "Lisa." That sitcom spoof of a city dweller who moved to a farm was a pretty accurate description of us. I was willing, however, to humble myself and jump in to "get my feet wet." I knew of no other way. I began to search the local newspaper ads for cattle, and shortly found exactly what I was looking for. "Yearling Charolais Heifers for sale" the ad read. I had no idea what a "Charolais" was. I knew that a heifer meant female, but I was so ignorant that I had to look it up to make sure. There was a picture of a Charolais cow in the Encyclopedia. "Vicci, come look at this! They're White!" "Oh, they're pretty." she replied.

I immediately called and got the Farmer on the line. After agreeing on a price, I said "Ok, I'll take two of them. Can you deliver them for us?" I asked. After a slightly awkward silence, he said "Well, I suppose so. Usually our buyers show up with a trailer. Don't y'all want to see them first?" "Yeah, sure!" I said. We got directions to his Farm, and Vicci and I shortly showed up at his gate. The Farmer must have known what kind of a person he was dealing with when we climbed out of our BMW. He was very polite to us, if a little cautious. "Y'all from Atlanta?" he asked, as if there was any doubt. "Used to live there." I answered. "Now we live out here in Newton County." (I said this with just a hint of pride.) We picked out two of the "prettiest" heifers, and he loaded them into his trailer. I took careful mental notes on his cattle trailer, and added it to my growing list of "cattle equipment to buy." We pulled out, and he followed us back to our place. There was a large sign at the entrance of our driveway which said "Crossfire Farm," as I had named it. We stopped at the gate to the big pasture in front of our house. The Farmer got out of his truck, and I noticed him checking out our fencing. He turned to me and said "Is this where you want to unload them?" "Yep."

He opened the gate, and turned them loose. The Charolais took off, obviously glad to be free of the confines of the trailer, but a bit pensive about their new environment. I was not concerned – it was a large field with plenty of grazing. I settled up with the Farmer, and he drove off. Vicci and I stood back and proudly observed our two new French cattle in our own pasture. How satisfying. The cattle trotted off towards the woods on the North side of the field. "They're just exploring." I said to Vicci. Vicci wandered into the house, while I got out my ATV and procured a bag of Corn out of the Barn. I was going to feed my own cattle! I headed towards the woods where I had last seen them. "C'mon' cows!" I yelled. I drove back and forth, and didn't see them. "Where the heck are they?" I felt a little twinge of alarm. I raced along the edge of the woods. No sign of them. It was no longer a twinge. "Where are my new cattle?" I rode my ATV all the way around the trees to the North edge of my property. Then, I saw it. "Oh NO!" The barbed wire fence was down. I dismounted and walked up to the fence. "How in the blazes did this happen?" There was at least a 20 foot section of wire that was just lying on the ground. Plus, the wire was severely rusted, and the fence posts, which were wood, looked like they were 50 years old.

Panicked, I raced back to the house. I burst in the door, yelling "Vicci, Vicci! Our cows got out, and they are gone!" "Well where did they go?" she said. "Heck, I don't know. We've got to go find them!" We grabbed a section of rope. (I have no idea why. What did we think we were going to do with it?) We piled on the ATV and raced back out to the downed fence. "See" I said. "This is where they got out." When we first looked at the property, I noted that it was fenced, but I had neither the experience nor the know-how to tell that it badly needed re-fencing. Just then I heard a "moo." As I looked up, I saw two beautiful Charolais heifers contentedly munching on our neighbor's grass. Vicci and I cautiously got off the ATV, rope in hand. Slowly we ambled towards the cows, while chanting in our calmest tone of voice, "Here cows, here cows." The two cows just gave us a blank stare, as only a cow can. Suddenly they turned and briskly trotted away. We chased them for a while, getting further from our property line. Finally, it dawned on us that this was a task beyond our capability. "Honey, we've got to call somebody. We need help."

We had no clue who to call. I was too embarrassed to call the Farmer who sold us the cattle. One of my neighbors, Charlie Brown, came to our rescue. I knew Charlie from Church. He said "Kerry, you need to call Walt Weathers. He chases cows for a living." "Wow, thanks! I will!" I didn't care how much it cost. I just wanted my Charolais back. Immediately I called the number that Charlie gave me. A man, with a *very* heavy Georgia accent answered the phone. "Walt Weathers Cow Retrieval Service." "Sir," I said, "I need help. We just purchased two heifers, and they got out." "Where y'all at?" I told him our address and he said "Give me a few minutes to get everything together, and I'll be right over." I got the feeling he was a serious man who enjoyed his work.

About 20 minutes passed by before I heard a rumbling sound at the end of our driveway. The entrance to Crossfire Farm was a good quarter of a mile away, so this sound got my attention. Coming down the road was a most unusual, and curious looking rig. It was a big red "dually" truck pulling the longest trailer I had ever seen. This trailer had too many doors on it, or so I thought. It rolled to a stop in front of Vicci and I, and Mr. Weathers got out. His helper exited the other side. There was a commotion going on in his trailer – the excited baying of what sounded like Bloodhounds. He walked up to me, held out his hand, and introduced himself. "Walt Weathers." Some people have an instinct to perceive when they are in the presence of an extraordinary personality. I admit that occasionally I have that instinct, and at that moment it was working. Walt Weathers looked like the ultimate cow hand. He was a Southern version of "Crocodile Dundee." (Forgive me, Walt.) He looked at me for a second, as if to "size me up." I sensed that he knew exactly how much I knew about cattle – nothing. He asked if I knew where I had last seen my missing animals. "Sure do. Right over there." I said while pointing to the fence.

"All right." he said. "We'll look at that in a minute. First there's some things you need to know." I will never forget what he said next. He pointed his finger to the East. "If them cows is in there, I ain't goin' in there after 'em. There's things in there ain't never see folks." I thought that his delivery of this line was so Southern, and so quotable, that I just had to laugh. To really get it, it requires an explanation. The tract of land to our East was known as sort of a "No Man's Land." It was uninhabited, rough, and nearly impenetrable. It was a swamp. Walt Weathers knew this land, and he wasn't going near it. "Now that we got that understood, let me acquaint you with my rig." He began to show me what was behind those trailer doors. The first compartment contained tools and fencing supplies, all neatly stowed away. The second held his Weapons. He pulled out his Rifle, and showed me how he loaded it with Tranquilizer darts. The third door revealed two Horses, all saddled up and ready to go. He and his buddy unloaded them and tied them to the trailer, which had a convenient hitch. The next compartment contained the dogs, which had been making a racket. There was one compartment left, which obviously held a solitary dog. I knew this because he had a very different type of bark. "What's the deal with this dog?" I asked. He began to explain. "That's a Catahoula. We only let him out if everything else fails. If we do, I guarantee you'll be haulin' them dead cows to the slaughter house, or the buzzards will have 'em." My eyes grew wide.

So, the chase began. Walt and his helper pulled their truck up and opened the rear doors in such a way that it formed sort of a cattle pen. He had spotted the two cows in a pasture far to the north. (With Binoculars.) Astride their horses, they rode toward them. I followed on the AVT, observing at a safe distance. They were obviously attempting to corral the Charolais in the trailer. The cows knew what they were up to. They kept splitting up and running in opposite directions. This went on for a while, and was clearly frustrating Walt. I thought I heard him cussing, but I'm not sure. Eventually, the horsemen concentrated on one of the cows, and got her to run back towards the trailer. They got her in, and shut one of the inner doors. Walt took off after the remaining cow. She was clearly the bad influence on the other one. She just would not cooperate. She ran across the road and straight into a subdivision. This was exactly what I feared. Homeowners were watering their lawns, and having backyard barbecues as Walt disappeared from view among the houses. After a few minutes Walt reappeared, chasing the cow back in our direction. She ran to a remote part of the pasture and started grazing. He gave up the pursuit, trotted his horse up to us, and dismounted. "Got to go to phase II" he said, as he loaded up his Tranquilizer gun. "What happened in the subdivision?" I asked. He told me that one of the neighbors came out and started cussing him out. "We don't want your G** D*** cows in our yard!" Walt gave them a choice reply. "Well Mister, what do you think we're doing here? We don't want our cows in your yard either."

After a short chase, it was over. The lone Charolais had met her match in a dose of Tranquilizer. The Hounds, and the dreaded Catahoula, had not been needed. With the help of a winch, the heifer was loaded into the trailer. After loading the horses, Walt got into his truck, started the engine with its characteristic rumble, and drove the massive truck and trailer back to my property. The next hour or so, he and his buddy mended my fence – proper. I told him how much I appreciated his work, and especially for the "education in all things cattle." I wrote him a check, and he drove off into the Sunset. I don't remember how much Walt Weathers had cost me, but the price was well worth it, it more ways than one. There is always lessons to be learned. Here they are.

Mistake # 1: Never start a cattle operation with Charolais, or any other pure-bred exotic breed.
Mistake # 2: Always check your fences before putting any live-stock on your land. Common sense.
Mistake # 3: If it is possible that a cow can get out, and even if it is not, they will.
Mistake # 4: A cow is not your pet dog. It won't come when you call it. (At least not initially.) Get help!

Recovered

"and in one gleaming moment I saw beyond the tomb"

In the Spring of 1998, I was home late one afternoon watching a Movie with my son, Kyle. It was a bit out of character for me to be viewing a DVD during the afternoon, but I was doing a bit of babysitting. We were watching "Tombstone." My wife, Vicci, had left us to attend a "Mother-Daughter Banquet." Along with her was Phyllis Chan, an exchange student from Hong Kong, who we were hosting that year. Our daughter, Katy, was acting in a play at Cair Paravel Latin School where she attended. Vicci was very proud of Katy's performance, especially since she had been a Theater Arts Major in college. After the banquet was over, Vicci made a last minute decision to swing by a local super-market (Bauersfeld's) to get a dozen roses for Katy. She was always doing stuff like this, so I wouldn't have given it a second thought.

The roses were never to arrive. Vicci parked her car in a slot, and began walking toward the door of the market. At the same moment, a teenage girl put her car in reverse, and, for some unexplainable reason floored it. Vicci never knew what hit her. The impact sent her airborne, and she landed on the back of her head on the curb. It was not a soft landing. One of the witnesses, a Vietnam Veteran, said it was one of the worst things he had ever seen. Phyllis had witnessed the entire event, and had run over to a bank of payphones to try to call me. She tried to ask people for help, but was so traumatized that she couldn't remember her English. Another witness happened to be another girl from Katy's School, Amy Brown. She had a cell phone. Being a friend of Katy's she had our phone number, and immediately called our home number. The phone rang, and I got up from the couch, grumbling something to myself about my movie being interrupted. There was a very excited female voice on the other end which said "Mr. Livgren, your wife has been hit by a car." I thought it was some sort of prank, until I heard the ambulance sirens over the phone. "Where?" I stam-

69

mered. "In the parking lot at Bauersfeld's. They're taking her to Stormont Vail I think." (Stormont Vail is a local Hospital) Phyllis got on the phone, but she was so distressed that she kept lapsing into Chinese. I abruptly hung up the phone.

It took about two seconds to sink in, and I launched into "emergency mode." I grabbed Kyle, and set a new land speed record getting from our farm to the hospital. On the way there, my mind was filled with thoughts about how much I loved my wife. Scenes of our past floated by. The horror of facing life without her filled my mind, followed by urgent prayers. I pulled up at the entrance to the emergency room, and walked inside. Strangely, there were several familiar faces there – from our Church. Apparently, word had gotten around at the School, which was just blocks away. Kyle didn't know what was going on. Poor little guy, he was sobbing. A lady grabbed him and ushered him off to one of the waiting rooms. Someone else took my arm and led me to the front desk. There, you are supposed to have all your Insurance information – the last thing you want to think about. I just wanted to see my wife.

Then a guy dressed in "scrubs" came up to me, looked me in the eye, and said "Mr. Livgren, in a moment, we will let you see your wife. I have some information for you." He handed me a pamphlet. I don't remember much about it, except it dealt with "Living with a Severe Head Injury." Then he walked off. My head was reeling. I just didn't seem to be able to process this information. Now stick with me here. This is where it starts to get really interesting. As I stood in line, someone tapped me on the shoulder. I turned around, and there was another young man standing directly behind me. He had blonde hair, and I remember he also was wearing "scrubs." I recall that his eyes looked intense, but at the same time they were comforting. He said, in a soft voice, "Don't worry, she's going to be all right." Then he walked away. Before I had time to react, someone else said "Mr. Livgren? You can see your wife now." A nurse led me into a curtained room, and there she was, lying on a Gurney. Vicci was clearly conscious – but not in the way I wanted her to be. There was spinal fluid and blood coming out of both her ears. She was looking somewhere else, and did not recognize me. She was having a very animated conversation with someone I could not see. I could not understand all of what she was saying, but I got the gist of it. She kept saying "But I don't want to go back! Please don't make me go back." In the current context, it made no sense. It would later. Then the nurses came and wheeled her out of the room. A distinguished looking man, who was clearly a Doctor, introduced himself as "Dr. Yorke." He said "We are going to get some CT images." He gave me instructions on how to get to the waiting room on the proper floor.

The following hours are pretty much a blur. I was so stunned, that I could do little but pace the floor. A young assistant Pastor from our Church, Doug Simmons, became my companion. I remember Dr. Yorke coming into the room and saying "The back of her skull is fractured in so many pieces, we can't put it together again. We'll just observe her for now." The hours wore on, intermixed with sleep and prayer. Doug never slept, bless his heart, he just kept praying. I was still stunned. The faint light of dawn was beginning to appear in the window. I remembered that this was a Saturday night, now Sunday morning. At about 10am, a nurse suddenly opened the door, and exclaimed "Mr. Livgren, she's waking up! She's waking up!" I did not know if she would ever wake again. Startled, I jumped up off of the floor where I was sleeping and ran to where she directed me. There was Vicci, sitting upright. There were all sorts of wires and monitors hooked up to her, which she was unceremoniously disconnecting. "What's all this stuff? What happened to me?" she said. I wanted to jump and shout. The nurse said "I'll get Dr. Yorke."

The Doctor soon appeared. "Hmmm...well this is a good sign!" Then he put her CT scan up on a viewer. He showed me exactly where the brain damage was. Even I could see it. "I think this scan can't be correct. Let's get another one." The second one proved to be the same as the first one. Later, after getting a third image, the brain damage shown on the first two was not present. I said "Doctor, what's going on?" Dr. Yorke said "Well, the word "Miracle" is not in our Medical Terminology, but sometimes things like this happen which we can not explain." Sweeter words I never heard.

Vicci came home, and slowly resumed her life. The only lasting symptom of this incident is that her sense of smell is diminished. I found out some additional information about that night, and the following morning. Several members of Topeka Bible Church had been praying in the Hospital Chapel throughout the whole ordeal. The congregation prayed for her in the Church Service that morning – at the exact moment she woke up. And who was the young man in scrubs who declared that she was, in spite of her Medical condition, going to be all right? Who was the invisible person that Vicci was having the conversation with in the Emergency Room? Personally, I think I know beyond any shadow of doubt.

Kerry's First Bus Ride

The members of "White Clover," who were soon to become "Kansas," did not have any "hazing" traditions for new members, but they might as well have instituted at least one. When I decided to leave the band I was playing in and join "White Clover" I might have thought otherwise about that decision had I known what they had in store for me.

It was their bus. It was a worn out late Sixties model School bus. I had driven plenty of hours in School buses in previous bands, but this one was a bit unique. The entire thing was painted black. All the rear seating had been removed to make room for the band's equipment, leaving only a few rows of seats in the front. It had been named. That's right, it had a name. "Corn Woman." The band had seen the movie "Little Big Man" starring Dustin Hoffman. One of the characters in the film was named "Corn Woman," and for whatever reason, the name was applied to the bus. Don't look for any logic here...

After a couple of weeks rehearsing, with me learning their songs and them learning some of mine, it came time for our first gig. The band, however, was not yet comfortable playing the new songs, so it was decided that I would go along for the ride, but not actually play with them. I was a bit disappointed, but I understood. As we all climbed into "Corn Woman," Rich Williams was the driver. The gig was all the way out in Liberal, Kansas – a long drive. After a few hours of driving, we turned south off of I-70 onto a two-lane road. We had just driven a few miles, when Rich said "Time for somebody else to drive. Take over, Kerry." I was eager to prove myself, so I replied "Sure. I'll drive." This was a pretty deserted stretch of road, so Rich just pulled off to the side. The band members were all watching me, as if I was about to discover something *very* interesting. I slid into the driver's seat, put the bus in gear, and pulled onto the highway. Then I discovered "it." "Whoa!" I yelled.

"What's going on here?" The steering wheel was going haywire. It was so loose that it was barely functional. I was weaving back and forth all over the road. They were all hooting. "Give it time, you'll get the hang of it." someone said. Apparently, the guys had been driving it in this condition for some time. Well, true to their word, it did stabilize after a while, but it took constant vigilance on my part. "Oh, and watch out for the brakes." said Rich. "They might take some muscle." "What a surprise." I thought.

At that moment we crested a pretty large hill (yes, there are hills in Kansas) and started down. I was preoccupied with keeping the bus steady. When I looked ahead, I noticed something that really caught my attention. There were train tracks at the bottom of the hill. A fraction of a second later, we all heard the unmistakable horn of a Locomotive. I looked to my left and saw the Freight Train barreling straight for our intersection. Simultaneously, every-one of us screamed. We were all yelling stuff like "Oh, My God, it's going to hit us!" and "We're all dead men!" Instinctively, I stepped on the brakes – nothing. Half-panicked, I began pressing on the brakes with both feet. Ever so slowly we began to slow down. Being on a big downward slant did not help the process. "We're not going to make it!" yelled someone. I got into a half-standing position and put all the weight and strength I had on that pedal. Gradually, the bus slowed and stopped, just three feet from the speeding train. We all sat there in stunned silence as the train sped by. With the exit of the Caboose, came an eruption of ner-vous, hysterical laughter. We all looked at each other, amazed and relieved to be alive. My hands were shaking. "I'm through driving this thing!" I exclaimed.

Robby Steinhardt was the proud owner of a small battery-powered Sony Cassette recorder. He had made several recordings of White Clover and Kansas with this amazing little machine. When things settled down and we got back on the road, Robby says "Hey guys, listen to this!" He had the whole thing on tape. I could not believe that, in all that panic, he had the presence of mind to turn on his recorder. There it was, with all our screaming and everything.

Robby had recorded this near-death miracle. If he could ever locate that cassette, I think we would have another hit on our hands!

The Strange Instruments of My Youth

I had the privilege of being exposed to some very interesting and unusual musical instruments in my youth. When I was very young, I perceived them to be toys, as I was not prohibited from "playing" them. Playing, to me, meant making noise. One of the primary noise-makers was the old Upright Piano in the basement of our house. For some reason now lost, my Father had spray-painted the Antique Piano with a bright green speckled paint. I suppose he thought that the original finish was beyond repair. Besides, these old Pianos were a dime a dozen, literally. If we didn't like it, it could have been easily replaced. Even today, you can probably find one of them free, as long as you agree to haul it away.

I sat at the bench of that Piano for countless hours, first just banging on the keys, and eventually making some sounds that might actually be described as Musical. Eventually, my parents decided that I should have Piano lessons. First, there was Mr. Blem, and then there was Mrs. Whitsell. I don't remember much about Mr. Blem's lessons, except being frustrated. At the time, I would much rather have been playing baseball, or flying a Kite. Making Music should not have to be so much work. I do remember Mrs. Whitsell, however. She was a kind, elderly lady who knew much more than she let on. The first few lessons involved learning to read sheet Music. She would place a Music Book on the Piano and ask me to play one of the selections. I would then ask her if she would play it for me first, just so I could hear it. Of course, what was going on was a bit of deception on my part. I would watch her fingers as she played, while listening intently to the music. Then I would attempt to play it, usually with some success. Why should I have to read it off a page when I could understand it perfectly by listening to it?

Wise old Mrs. Whitsell knew exactly what was happening. From the very beginning, I just didn't "get" reading Music. It was a classic case of "Playing by Ear." Mrs. Whitsell tried to teach me, but eventually she spilled the beans to my Mom. "Kerry has a great gift for Music, but he's just not doing well with reading musical notation." That was the end of Piano lessons. My parents thought that perhaps I just didn't like the Piano, so they bought me a Clarinet. My Grade School offered musical Training in those days, so I could play in the School Orchestra. They bought me a Silver instrument, the inexpensive kind used by students who played in marching bands. I did make some attempts at playing it that only resulted in horrible squawks, and I still had to read the notes off a page. My career with the Clarinet lasted about three weeks. By the time I got to Junior High School, I was a Drummer. My parents had bought me a set of Drums, which I thought was really cool, and I could play them pretty well, but then at last I discovered the Guitar, and the rest is history.

A Piano is not an unusual instrument, and neither is a Clarinet, but what my Dad had attached to that Upright Piano in the basement was. There was a small electric Keyboard instrument which slid underneath the Piano's Keyboard. It was called a Clavioline. When I say small, I'm not kidding. The keys were about half the length of a Piano key, and the Keyboard itself was just short of three octaves, but Oh, what fun it was to play! (Obviously, my interest in the Piano had been rekindled by this time.) Long before the days of Synthesizers, the Clavioline was on the cutting edge of Electronic Instruments. It had a small tube amplifier which sat next to the Piano, and the Clavioline itself had a number of switches on the front of it, which were for selecting different sounds. It could make the most unique and haunting sounds I had ever heard, and its Vibrato was unmistakable. (You can hear one on the Keyboard solo on "Runaway" by Del Shannon, or "Telstar" by the Tornados.) My Dad used to sit at the Piano, and play it with his left hand, and the Clavioline with his right. I had no idea where my Father found it, but my guess is he got it at my Uncle Ole's Music Store. The Clavioline, (and my Dad and Uncle), were clearly ahead of their time! Uncle Ole was a life-long Musician, and for many years he had played live every morning on Topeka's WIBW radio. He was a master of the Hammond Organ and the Accordion. He loved to tinker with electronics. Arguably, the most famous of his inventions was the "Olevox." It was a bit before my time, so I can't describe exactly what it was. It was some sort of electrified instrument that used an Accordion to play other musical sounds. He performed with it several times on the Radio, and apparently people were quite amazed by it. When he retired, he opened his Music Store. He primarily sold Lowrey Organs, but that is where my Dad purchased my first "store-bought" Guitar, a Kay Hollow Body with a single Pickup.

In 1959, Uncle Ole went to California to the NAMM Show. It was there that he first saw it – the Chamberlin. The Chamberlin was an electronic Keyboard instrument that was the forerunner to the Mellotron. At the time, it was *way* ahead of its time, and being Uncle Ole, it was right up his alley. The Chamberlin was an ingenious contraption in which the keys triggered a series of audio tapes. The tape banks contained everything from Band and Orchestral instruments to sound effects. It was about the same size as a Hammond B3, and it was a very heavy instrument. I don't know how Uncle Ole got it back to Topeka. He immediately set up a "demonstration" of it in his store. My Mom and Dad were there, as well as my cousins Larry and Linda. Larry was a musician as well. Uncle Ole sat down at the instrument and began to play. Everyone's mouth dropped open, including my Dad's. It was as if an entire Brass Band was playing in front of us, with all the supporting instruments such as Guitar, Bass, and Drums. How could this be? Next came a String Section and Woodwinds. We were totally amazed. Uncle Ole was smiling from ear to ear. Then Larry got up and played a song. (He had apparently been practicing on it from the moment it arrived.) I remember Larry played a song which featured Trombone sounds, but then he had us all laughing when he pressed a key and we heard Chickens clucking, a Rooster crowing, and Ducks quacking. The evening was full of wonders. It was as if we had suddenly been given a glimpse of the future, and in a way we had. Not until the 1980's, when the Emu "Emulator I" came out, would I have access to such sounds. Larry reportedly played some local "lounge" gigs with the Chamberlin, but that was the last I heard of it.

In the early Seventies, when I was with the second Kansas Band (later known as Proto-Kaw), I began wondering what had ever become of my Uncle's Chamberlin. I wanted a Mellotron in the worst way, but had no hope of affording one. The more I thought about it, the more interested I became. Uncle Ole passed away in 1969, but my Aunt Jane was still living, so one day I gave her a call and asked her about it. She said "Kerry, I don't know, but I think it's here in the house somewhere. You're certainly welcome to it." Wow! I immediately went to her house with one of our roadies and picked it up. I made that sound too easy. It was a bit weightier than I had imagined. The heavy wood cabinet, and the big wooden cylinder inside accounted for most of the weight, but we managed to muscle it into our truck. After unloading it very carefully into the living room of our band house, I stood back and surveyed this wondrous Musical Instrument. I had a Chamberlin! My mind raced with fantasies about its effect on our band. We would be known far and wide! Little did I know how frustrating it would be. I had no idea how to operate it. I certainly could play a Keyboard, but this was different, and it did not come with a Manual. To start with, I had to clean off the dust which had accumulated from years of storage in my Uncle's house. With that done, I held my breath and flipped the switch. When the tubes warmed up, I heard a low hum – a good sign. I selected a String bank, the one I was most interested in, and pressed a key. A scratchy, warbly, sound came out. Obviously, it had once been some sort of String instrument, but now it was mostly noise. Clearly, something was wrong. For the next week, I spent hours trying to decipher what the problem was. I removed the back panel, which gave me access to all of the tapes. The tapes were wound around a cylindrical wooden capstan, and for some reason they were getting all fouled up, and worse, the oxide was coming off of the tapes. I tried cleaning them up, but the more I tried, the more fouled up they became. Eventually, I discovered what was wrong, when I found an extremely sticky substance on my fingers, something like sap. It *was* sap! Over time, that wooden capstan had secreted sap all over the tapes, ruining them. Even if I was able to find the manufacturer, I was sure the cost of replacing all of the tape banks, the capstan, the pressure pads, the tape heads, and the pinch rollers, would be prohibitive for my meager budget. The Chamberlin was reduced to being a fascinating piece of furniture, but otherwise it was a wreck. Thus, my dreams of having the one of the most unique musical instruments ever made were just "Dust in the Wind." I would just have to make my music in more conventional ways. My fascination with interesting and unusual musical instruments didn't end, however. It continues to this day, but I am sure I will probably never know the wonders of musical instruments like the Clavioline and the Chamberlin again.

XXX and the Bomb

note: This story partially relies on memories other than my own. As near as I can tell, the story is totally factual – but then possibly not...

In the early days of touring with Kansas we mostly opened the show for headlining acts, but occasionally we would play Rock clubs. One such establishment was in the suburbs of Chicago. (Unfortunately, I have forgotten its name.) We played many such clubs, and always got a raucous and enthusiastic reception. Some of those enthusiastic fans were members of a local band who had seen us play in the Chicago area, and were quite impressed with us. They were impressed by our song-writing and our musicianship, but what really got to them was the "flash bombs" we used at the end of our show. They had never seen anything like this. Their band will heretofore be referred to as "XXX," since I can't remember their name. (Sorry!) Kansas began using these "bombs" a few months earlier. If they are loaded with the right amount of flash powder they are mostly harmless. Jerry Gilleland, our stage manager, was given that task. Except for the time one of the bombs set Robby's hair on fire at a gig in Atlanta, the bombs had a flawless reputation!

From this point on, this tale I am telling relies upon the recollection of the Club's manager, who relayed it to us the next time he saw us. Apparently XXX was so blown away by the Kansas concert experience, that they immediately went home, learned a Kansas song, and ordered two Flashbombs from a local Theater Supply company. Since they lived in Chicago, the bombs arrived shortly, and the band could hardly contain their excitement. They immediately contacted the club owner, who was acquainted with them, and secured a booking for the next week. As they were playing their set, the excitement was building. The Kansas song was approaching on their set list. What the band members didn't know, was that pride leads to a fall. Earlier, they had called a band meeting, and had come up with a plan to supersede what Kansas had

81

done. They told their Roadie to fill the bomb canisters "to the max." Normally, it takes only a small amount of flash powder – just enough to cover the small copper wire fuse. I have no idea how much powder "to the max" consisted of, but clearly they didn't read the instructions.

The moment came. The Kansas song reached its ending crescendo. In their wildest imagination, no one, including the band members, could suspect what happened next. The Roadie threw the switch. In the (approximate) words of the Club owner, "Suddenly all I could see was brilliant whiteness. The next thing I was able to perceive was the Singer and Bass player flying end over end across the room. Everyone in the club hit the floor. When the smoke cleared, there was musical debris all over the place. The Drum Kit was destroyed. Mic stands and Amps were lying around in disarray. The miracle was, apart from a bunch of ringing ears, no one was seriously hurt."

I don't know whatever became of "XXX," but I do know this – they sure "superseded" Kansas on that night!

The Gloworm

God *must* have a sense of humor. The experience of being human almost demands it, and He certainly created us with the capacity for laughter. This thought was brought to mind by an incident I remember back in 1982. In those days, I would frequently return home late at night from a tour, or a recording session. Vicci would have long since gone to bed, and I would try to slip stealthily into the bedroom without waking Katy, our baby daughter.

On this particular occasion, I did just that. I turned the bedroom light off, and was just drifting off to sleep when I sensed that something was different. As I opened my eyes, a strange soft light was emanating from the hallway. I bolted upright. There was an eerie glow, flickering and moving slowly toward our bedroom, as if someone, or *some thing*, was carrying a candle and walking towards us. I went on "full alert" and the hair stood up on the back of my neck. The "strange glow" suddenly morphed into a floating human-like figure, which was advancing down our hallway in the most ghost-like fashion. My "full alert" status was now "full adrenaline alarm."

Facing the specter of some sort of malevolent spirit, I resorted to pure spiritual instinct. I leaped up, pointed my finger at it, and shouted in the most authoritative voice I could come up with. "In the name of Jesus, BE GONE!!" The figure shuddered, and I heard this sweet little voice say "Daddy?" Then the "ghost" fell on the floor, still emitting its light, and my little daughter came running and jumped into my arms. I was completely bewildered. What the heck? A bedside lamp came on, and I looked at my wife, who had just been so rudely awakened. I must have "looked a sight" to her - a mixture of scared to death and totally relieved.

Vicci looked at the "ghost" lying face down on the floor. When she realized what had just happened, she couldn't stop laughing. "You want to let me in on the joke?" I said. She explained to me that she had just purchased a new toy for Katy that day. The "Gloworm." It was sort of a little doll, with a battery powered head that glowed when it was squeezed. Katy had held it before her as she navigated toward the bedroom, which gave the appearance of its "floating" down the hall. Vicci said the "Gloworm" was the latest popular craze.

Well, it almost made *me* crazy. I had expended all of the spiritual energy I had for one night. As soon as the adrenaline wore off, I couldn't go to sleep for laughing. God *must* have a sense of humor.

The Lightning Machine Story
as told by Kerry Livgren in some interview...

I think we've got "Spinal Tap" (the Movie) beat. When Kansas was preparing for the 1977 Point of Know Return tour, we decided "We've got to have something in our live show that nobody's ever had." In those days the big arena-rock groups were very competitive. (As far as I know, they still are.)

We wanted to do something really different and unique that would absolutely dazzle our audiences. We didn't want to do the usual stuff – smoke bombs, strobes, lighting specials, etc., so we put the word out to the production companies that Kansas wanted something really different. Eventually a company (from somewhere in Texas as I recall) contacted us, and they said "Look you guys, we think we've got exactly what you need. You have a song on your new album called "Lightning's Hand." We've invented a Lightning Machine that will make controllable bolts of lightning in the concert hall!" When we heard this, we knew we had to have it. So, we rented this huge warehouse down by the Atlanta airport, and we called them and said "OK, you guys bring the machine down here, and we'll set up the band. Let's try this thing out." We showed up on the appointed day, and these guys pulled up in a big truck. They backed it up to the warehouse, opened the door, and down the ramp rolled this huge object on dollies, covered with a black tarp.

Our adrenaline was already pumping. They brought it into the warehouse, unveiled it, and there stood this huge ominous mechanism. We were riveted. It looked like something out of a Jules Verne novel – it had a huge black cone, and it had big electrodes all over it. The device looked just like the machines in a Franken-stein movie. Very foreboding. I remember thinking that this machine looked so cool that I didn't even care if it didn't do anything. It looked awesome just sitting there. We could hardly contain our excitement. They threw a big switch to turn it on, and you could hear this thing cranking up like a dynamo. The electrodes started to emit a sound like "bzzzt, bzzzt," with massive arcs of crackling blue-white electricity. Smaller tendrils of voltage were snaking all over the cone. You could smell the ozone as we started to back away.

We were all standing there, just transfixed at this spectacle, as the technician walked up to Robby. (Robby was the vocalist who sang "Lightning's Hand.") He said "OK, what you do is you hold this sword in your hand. There's a cord that runs out of the sword, down your pant-leg, and out past your foot so you're grounded." Then he says "When you get to that line in the song where you say 'I command the lightning's hand!' you hold the sword out away from you. We'll flip the switch, and the bolt of lightning will jump across the stage and hit your sword and go right out through the cord. You won't feel a thing." Robby looked white as a ghost, but at the same time he was excited to try it. Delusions of Grandeur...

We were all thinking "Man, this is going to be great! Styx and Journey, eat your hearts out!" All of a sudden the guy turns up the power on the machine, and Robby's big mountain of hair starts sticking straight up and moving all over the place. He looked like Medusa! The air was crackling as the Lightning Machine began vibrating and spitting out bursts of wattage. "Don't worry!" the operator yelled. "It's only static electricity." With his eyes as big as saucers and sweat trickling down his brow, Robby timidly crouched down and held out the sword as the music got louder. Just when he got to that line in the song, the technician threw a switch and the prophesied bolt of lightning jumped out. CRACK!!! It hit Robby right on the neck, and knocked him down to the ground! He's lying there, writhing around on the ground, and this thing's going "bzzzt, bzzzt, bzzzt." We were screaming "SHUT IT OFF! SHUT IT OFF!" I thought, "Oh, my God, he's dead!" Well obviously Robby survived, but it scared the devil out of him, (and us.) The technician apologized profusely. As it turns out, the ground plug had worked its way loose.

After "working the kinks out", we tried the infamous Lightning Machine at only one concert. It was the first show of the Point of Know Return tour. The concert was in Florida, as I recall. We started playing "Lightning's Hand" with much anticipation. The audience was enraptured when the machine was unveiled on its riser behind the drum kit. The moment came. We turn on the Lightning Machine, and it began it's arcing and "bzzzt, bzzzt" routine. Suddenly, KA-BLAM!!! It had caused a short-circuit and had blown out about half the speakers in the PA. The audience was bewildered. They didn't know what they had just seen, but they were *very* impressed. The bad news was – we had to stop the show. It was over. We apologized and left the stage. In retrospect, the Lightning Machine was *such* a cool idea, but we just couldn't make it work. I'd love to know whatever became of that thing.

Bus Tales

Every band that has spent any time in a Bus is going to have some "Bus Tales." It's inevitable. Here are a few of mine.

1. Late one night, while driving down Highway 75 after a gig in a Club in Holton, Kansas, we began to hear a strange noise. Strange noises were common in our old School Bus, but this one was *really* strange. It was a very rhythmic banging. It started out very subtle, almost inaudible, and then progressed to the level where it was unmistakable. We all heard it. All conversation stopped, as we looked at each other. We were all thinking the same thought. "What the heck is that?" The sound became mesmerizing, as it slowly grew in volume and intensity. The banging got so loud, we thought the Bus was going to explode. Then, in an instant, it was gone. The Bus was back to normal. We all breathed a sigh of relief – temporarily. But a few minutes passed, and it was back. This time it was the same rhythmic pattern of thumping, then banging, although the tone was a little different. Again it started out very softly, then grew loud. This time it was almost deafening. It was so ridiculous, we started laughing. "*What is it?*" Then again, it instantly stopped. All of our combined knowledge of things mechanical could not explain this mysterious noise.

One more time the whole cycle repeated. Bang, bang, bang, bang, BANG! It had a slightly different tone than before, then very abruptly stopped. Curiously, the Bus was silent the rest of the way home, but it seemed to drive slightly different, as if it was leaning slightly to one side. The mystery was solved as soon as we pulled into a Service Station. As we got out of the Bus, the unmistakable odor of burned rubber hit our nostrils. We could never afford a truly new manufactured tire. Instead we opted for Re-Treads, as they were much less expensive. One of our rear tires had started coming apart, layer by layer, and banging on the wheel-well. We left a trail of tread all the way down Highway 75. Makes a good Bus Tale, though.

2. Harmonic Balancer. I had never heard of one, nor even heard the term before. I was about to. While returning from a weekend concert somewhere in the wilds of Western Kansas, the engine of our old bus starting running rough. I mean *really* rough. It sounded as if it was about to fly apart, and was rapidly losing power. We pulled off to the side of I-70, with cars speeding past and trying to avoid the bulky School Bus. We held a Pow-Wow using our combined mechanical knowledge to try to figure out what was happening. No dice. We totally struck out. We were stranded, and the question was – what were we going to do about it? We decided that one of us was going to hitch-hike to the next gas station and call one of our friends to come get us. All except me, that is. The Band had promptly held an election, and I was the clear winner, or loser depending on your perspective. Somebody had to stay in the bus overnight and watch over all our equipment. Hooray. I think it was Rich or Dave, or perhaps both, that caught a ride into Topeka. Shortly thereafter a car arrived back at the bus to pick up the rest of the band. They half-jokingly wished me a good night, and off they went.

It was one of the worst nights that I ever spent anywhere. There was absolutely nothing to do, no radio, no TV, nothing to read, no one to talk to. There were trucks whizzing by every few seconds which made the bus rock back and forth. That made it very difficult to sleep. Sleep was nearly impossible anyway since my choices were either lying on one of the bench seats (which were entirely too short), or crawling back on the equipment and trying to find a level spot. To make matters worse, all I had for covers was a dusty tarp. Miserable. To their credit, Rich and Dave showed up fairly early to rescue me. Along with them came a Mechanic in his truck. He immediately opened the hood and started snooping and poking around. When he emerged, he said "Well, guys, it looks like your harmonic balancer is bad." "Pardon me," I said, our *what* is bad?" (We thought sure he was joking with us, because we were

89

just dumb musicians.) "Your harmonic balancer." he said. He then proceeded to attempt to educate us with an explanation. All I remember was that he used phrases like "torsional damper" and "rotating assembly." None of it made any sense to us. All we knew was that it was extremely inconvenient (especially for me), and that it was surely going to cost us big bucks. As it turned out, it was not that horribly expensive. The bus spent a day in the shop and was restored to us. I swear, none of us had ever heard of a "harmonic balancer," nor have I heard one mentioned since then. Maybe they were a rare part that was only installed on buses that belonged to Musicians.

3. On this night, Dave and I had bus driving duty. Dave's function, since he had no Driver's License, was to make conversation and keep the one who was actually driving awake. We were coming across Southwestern Kansas about 2 in the morning in the middle of a blinding blizzard. The rest of the guys were attempting to sleep in the back of the bus. I kept slowing the bus down, and peering into the windshield to try to see where I was going. The snowflakes were hypnotizing. Dave did his best to help me see, but between us we could barely make out the road.

Suddenly, we both hit the deck. A huge mysterious shape had just flown out of the darkness and nearly hit our windshield. It seemed to stretch the entire width of the bus. Dave and I looked at each other and we both had the same thought. "It was an Owl, a Great Snowy Owl!" Neither one of us had ever seen one, except in a book. Occasionally they are seen in the State of Kansas, but not often, that is, unless you are a member of a rock band in an old School bus in the middle of the night.

New Orleans Bike Ride

I loved recording at Studio in the Country. Bill Evans, its owner, had created his dream – a State of the Art recording studio in his home town, Bogalusa, Louisiana. The problem was, it was in the middle of a bayou in Bogalusa, Louisiana. To my knowledge, the only "name" artist to share his peculiar vision was Kansas. We loved it. We were there to record our third album, "Masque." I had decided to make kind of an adventure out of it. Well, more than the usual adventure, anyway. I made plans to ride my motorcycle, a Suzuki 750, from Atlanta down to Bogalusa. The trip went well. My companion on the ride was the brother of one of our roadies. Vicci wanted to come be with me during the recording, so I arranged a flight for her to join me. Our days in Bogalusa were quite memorable once Vicci got used to the local Paper Mill. If you've ever smelled that pungent aroma, you know of what I speak. You just had to ignore your nostrils and put it out of your mind. In spite of this, one of our favorite things to do there was each lunch at the Hotel Diner downtown. It was from another era. We always smiled when the Southern ladies would ask us, in their unmistakable accent, "Y'all want some pie?" We always did.

One day, when there was a lull in recording, (the board was always breaking down) I got the bright idea to ride on the Lake Pontchartrain Causeway down to New Orleans and spend the evening in the French Quarter, then ride back. The Causeway is a 24-mile long bridge which links Mandeville with Metairie, La. From there, it's just a short hop to New Orleans. We arrived about dusk and parked the bike. Bourbon Street was in full swing. It's impossible not to be impressed, whether you love it or hate it. There they were – mobs of people, all whooping it up, imbibing, and "painting the town red." Personally, I have always had sort of a morbid fascination with Bourbon Street – in small doses. I've had a few moments of weakness, but I have never been much for drinking and partying.

I'd be just as happy sitting on one of the covered porches above, and watching the festivities below.

Vicci and I took a couple of seats in one of the open front bars, and ordered a couple of Mint Juleps. The sound of multiple bands playing at once was maddening, but somehow appropriate. As we were finishing our drinks, I was rapidly approaching my "small dose" limit of Bourbon Street. It was time to depart. We paid our tab, and as we stepped outside on the street a passerby looked at Vicci, sized her up, and made an extremely lewd comment. Not only am I not much of a drinker, I'm not much of a fighter either. But this guy made me see red. My fists automatically formed up, and instantly I was in the guy's face. We were both yelling and about to come to blows, when along came my rescuing Angel, Vicci. She somehow got between us, and managed to soothe the tempers. Now it was *really* time to leave.

We began working our way through the crowd, to get back to where the Motorcycle was parked. Suddenly, I noticed someone who seemed utterly incongruous in this environment. He was a block away from us. He was a Street Preacher, one of those rare individuals who are called to Evangelize all the sinners to be found (in abundance) on Bourbon Street. He was a sight. He was waving his arms, jumping up and down, and preaching the Gospel with everything he had. While still a block away, he slowly turned his head and fixed his gaze directly on me. He fell silent for a few seconds, and then began preaching – at me. Me. "Why me?" I thought. "With all the transgressors and evildoers all around you, you have to preach at me?" From our current location, there was no way to get where we wanted to go except to walk right past him. As we drew near, his pontificating grew louder and more animated. I had never heard such Hellfire and Brimstone sermonizing directed at me. As we walked past, he actually began pleading with us, and reached out and grabbed my shirt. "Hey Man, cut it out! Enough already!" I yelled. My blood was still up from the near-fight, and I was in no mood. He kept on preaching at us as we walked away. The sound faded in the distance.

Our evening in the French Quarter was ruined. Vicci and I felt completely deflated. It was hard to forget that Street Preacher. Why did that guy single me out and start preaching at me? We walked to the Bike in silence. With my mind dwelling on the things that he had said, we mounted up and rode back to Bogalusa. Nearly ten years later, circumstances had brought me back to New Orleans. I went down to The Quarter just to walk around. I was moved. Now a Christian, I saw it through different eyes. I wondered "Who was that young Street Preacher?" I wonder what he would think, if he knew I was writing about him now. I have an idea...

Dan and the Exploding Carp

Dan Wright and I met in High School. We soon found out that he and I were kindred spirits, as we shared interest in nearly everything, especially music. On one occasion, we went over to his house, which was just across the street from our School, and he played for me the latest album that he had bought – Pet Sounds. Everyone had heard the Beach Boys, but this album was *so* different. Thus began my life-long infatuation with the Beach Boys.

Although Dan was not a Musician when I met him, he was shortly, (and somewhat reluctantly), to become one. In the early days of our "Musician-hood," the criteria was familiarity rather than musical ability. My "garage" band, the Gimlets, consisted of two Guitarists, a Bass player, and a Drummer. We needed a keyboard player in the worst way. Being in short supply, I decided that Dan was our man. The fact that he knew nothing about music and had never touched a keyboard was immaterial to me. I liked him! I presented him with the idea of joining our band. After an initial blank stare, he said "Me? I don't know how." "That's all right," I said. "I'll show you everything you need to know. It's easy." A glimmer of wonder came over his face, as he suddenly saw himself on stage. I knew it was a done deal.

Dan talked his Dad into loaning him the money to purchase an Organ. The only one he could afford was a very small Italian-made instrument, but man, that Organ was precious to him! I would show him how to play songs like "Louie, Louie" or "Shotgun," and he would practice and practice until he got it right. His first gig was at "Four Corners," a somewhat seedy night club a few miles south of Topeka. Technically, we shouldn't even have been there – we were too young. Dan was *really* nervous. When he got up on stage for his first performance, he set his fingers on the keyboard, and watched in horror as his instrument began rocking back and forth, and then tipped over and fell off the stage with a loud bang.

The Gimlets stopped playing and Dan just stood there looking hor-
rified and bewildered. So was the audience. Well, obviously his organ survived and Dan got over it. He went on to become a very tal-
ented Musician, and played with the first two versions of "Kansas." He is featured on the four albums released by "Proto-Kaw."

Now that you know some of the history of Dan and me, it's time to
get on with our tale. The Wright's owned a cabin at Lake Wabaunsee, located in the Flint Hills southwest of Topeka. I was very familiar with this Lake because my Uncle Ole also had a cabin there.
It was just a few days before the Fourth of July, and Dan invited
me to celebrate at the Lake with him. Fireworks are legal in the
State of Kansas, but not quite as legal as they are in Missouri. In
particular, you could buy M-80's in Missouri, but not in Kansas.
An M-80 was a type of very large firecracker. It always looked and
sounded to me like a half-stick of dynamite. *Very* potent. To be
frank, I was a bit afraid of them. Somehow, Dan had procured a
box of Silver Salutes, (actually more powerful than an M-80), and
brought them back to Kansas. He opened the box and said "Let's
have some fun!" I didn't know if Dan's Dad knew about the Silver
Salutes, but I had a feeling that he probably didn't.

He began shooting them off, while I watched with my hands over
my ears. They made a very distinctive "K-BOOM!" sound when
they ignited. I was sure the cops were going to catch us, but then
we were way out in Wabaunsee County. There was probably not a
Sheriff's Deputy for miles. After the first few bombs went off, Dan
began to get more creative. "Watch this!" he said. He stuck his
hands down into the mud of the Lake bank, brought up a handful,
and fashioned it into a big ball. He kneaded it for a while, then
carefully inserted a Silver Salute into the center of the big mud ball
with the fuse sticking out. With a grin on his face he said "It's a
Depth Charge!" I was fascinated. We walked out to the end of the
dock. Dan lit the fuse, and pitched it into the Lake. A few seconds
went by, and we heard a soft "WHUMP!," that was followed by a
big jet of water shooting into the sky. "Cool! That was really cool!"
Dan said. "Let's do another one!" After the second "Depth-

Charge," the unexpected happened. Suddenly, a huge, ugly Carp floated to the surface. I mean, this fish was *big*. Clearly, this was the coolest way to fish!

Dan grabbed a long stick, and maneuvered the Carp over to the water's edge. With a bit of effort, he picked the fish up out of the water and laid it on the dock. We stared at it, gloating over our "catch." Dan had one Silver Salute left. With a twinkle in his eye, he again said "Watch *this*!" He carefully inserted it into the fish's mouth. Chuckling, he said, "We better take cover! Get over there behind the boathouse." He lit the fuse, and ran to join me. We peeked around the edge of the boathouse in eager anticipation. At that very second, Dan's Dad appeared. Apparently he had heard all the racket, and was curious what we were up to. He was walking directly towards us, but we were in hiding. Then he spied the Carp. He walked right up to it, and bent over it. Silver Salutes, for safety reasons, have a fairly long burning fuse. It seemed like an eternity. The fuse was crackling, and smoke was coming out of the fish's mouth. He bent closer. "What the..." K-BOOM!!

When the smoke cleared, Mr. Wright was standing there with the most bewildered look a man can possibly have. I think his brain was half in shock, and the other half was trying to process what just happened. His shirt and his pants were covered in fish scales and guts. They were even in his hair. His ears *had* to be ringing. Dan cautiously ambled up to him, and said something that I could not hear, but it looked like a frantic attempt to explain the incident. As Mr. Wright was listening to what he was saying, his expression slowly changed from incredulity to righteous anger. Dan backed up, then turned and ran like his life depended on it. (It probably did!) They ran up the embankment toward the cabin, his Dad right on his tail and yelling the whole way.

I was left standing alone, with that tremendously uncomfortable feeling you get when one of your friends gets in trouble with his parents. When they had disappeared around the corner of the cabin, I took the opportunity to make my exit. I hurriedly made my way to the 1961 Plymouth my parents had let me borrow, climbed in, and made my getaway. On the 40-mile drive back home, I had plenty of time to think. "Man, I bet Dan is really getting it!" Well, if he was, I suppose he deserved it. For that matter, so did I!

I Have So Much To Say, and Yet I Cannot Speak

It was a typical Monday morning in late summer. I had started the day with chores in the Barn and followed with a few hours in the Recording Studio. The lazy afternoon was so pleasant that I decided to give up the rest of the workday and fly one of my radio-controlled planes in the pasture. I had enjoyed exceedingly good health all my life, except for an occasional bout with a cold. After reaching 50, I was more vigilant, but there was never much need to see a doctor other than an occasional physical. My cholesterol and blood pressure were at normal levels, and I got plenty of exercise here at the farm. I thought I had nothing to worry about, but that was about to change.

I went to bed about ten-thirty that night, read a little bit and went shortly to sleep. From this point on, I remember little about that evening, which, in retrospect was God's mercy. It was about 3:30 in the morning. I remember waking up, and feeling *really* weird – in a way that I had never felt before. I rose and headed for the bathroom. After splashing some cold water on my face, the world started to spin and I dropped to the floor. I didn't know it, but a massive blood clot had just entered my left carotid artery, working its way toward my brain. After lying on the floor for an indeterminate amount of time, something awakened Vicci, my wife, who quickly called 911 thinking perhaps that I had suffered a heart attack. I have vague recollections of struggling unsuccessfully to get to my feet – and a feeling of bewilderment as to why the right side of my body would not function. Soon the paramedics arrived to take me to the hospital. I remember one of their faces staring down at me, but then I lost consciousness.

I was rushed to the Emergency Room, and from there to surgery at about seven o'clock. The surgeons strove to keep my arteries open, with some success. Two stents were placed in the blood vessel. Eventually I was to find out that, for a time, my life hung in the balance, but there on the operating table the balance swung in my favor. Despite the successful surgery however, later tests showed that a second blood clot had again blocked the carotid artery. There was not an attempt to remove this one – there was just too much mass of coagulation. To this day it remains completely blocked.

For the next three and a half days, I knew nothing. I was in a black vacuous void, lacking sound, sight, and feeling. Even when we are in normal sleep, we still have a sense of "self-presence." There is an awareness that though we are not conscious, we still exist. I was nowhere, totally beneath any level of consciousness. I began waking up, as if in a fog. I could see shadowy figures moving. My right side felt dead, and I couldn't speak. There had been dozens of friends and well-wishers in the emergency recovery room, but I can hardly remember their presence. Among them was Rob Raynor, my best friend from Georgia. He would play CD's of my favorite music for me, even when I was sleeping. Many of my friends were there praying for me, and they had notified many others that I'm not acquainted with who joined them in prayer.

I still didn't know what had happened to me. Unfortunately, in the days to follow, it did begin to dawn on me. My wife had been with me throughout the ordeal, and she began trying to tell me what had happened to me. She told me that I had suffered a stroke, and a very serious one. Initially I couldn't move my right arm or hand, but over the next several days I began to show some improvements such as wiggling my fingers and toes. My right leg was recovering more rapidly, and eventually I was able to stand upright. At one point, I remember Vicci was in the room, and one of my Doctors was holding up a small whiteboard on which he drew a picture with a marker. He was attempting to explain what had happened, and why that there was nothing more (surgically) that they could do for me. My mind was still foggy, but I understood what he was saying even if I couldn't comprehend the details.

The next day I had another visitor – Phil Ehart, the drummer for "Kansas." He had flown up to Topeka when he had heard what had happened to me. I recall that he took my hand and said something to me, but I still was not able to properly respond. Also, there were many friends from Topeka Bible Church who came, as well as members of my family. Later, Vicci told me that I had a constant stream of visitors, most of whom she had to (sadly) turn away. I don't know what the Doctors expected regarding my recovery, especially with that artery still blocked. I knew little about strokes – just what I had read, or heard from friends and family. I knew they were serious, even life threatening. I suppose, giving the nature of the malady, that anything was possible. Some recovery could take place, or none at all, but that was now in God's hands. Still, the improvements came, but it was tremendously frustrating, I began to be able to say a few understandable words, and I could now, with assistance, stand and walk some cautious steps. Therapists were now visiting me regularly and helping with speech and physical therapy. Some of my thought processes and memory were coming back. I remember desperately wanting to get better and be able to go home, but that was not yet to be. At one point Katy was wheeling me around the hospital in a wheelchair. Just to break up the monotony, I got her attention, and as we were nearing the elevator I whispered, urgently, "Katy! Katy! Hurry- let's make a break for it!!! Get the keys, let's get OUT OF HERE! Break me out!!"

After eleven days in Stormont Vail Hospital, the decision was made to move me to a Rehab facility. Several different places were discussed, but it was decided that I would be moved to Madonna Rehabilitation Hospital, a very respected clinic in Lincoln, Nebraska. I wanted to stay in Topeka, but I certainly was in no position to protest. Vicci wanted me to have the best care. After one more (rather lengthy) blood test, they loaded me in an ambulance and off I went. The scenery on the way up to Lincoln was very refreshing to me – the first I had seen in a long while. The clinic was very nice. I arrived late in the afternoon and was checked into an (almost) elegant room, right next to the dining room. At the call to dinner, I got up and tried to walk to the table, but a nurse stopped me. I was not allowed to walk to the dining table. I had to "graduate" into walking independently. They were afraid that I would stumble. The rest of the people were in wheelchairs. Most were considerably older than I, and many were obviously fellow stroke victims. You can usually tell them by their faces. I remember thinking that most of these people were hurting much worse than I. There wasn't much conversation at the table, presumably because of our shared vocal problems. The meal was very good, but I noticed, really for the first time, that I had great difficulty holding the fork. I had previously been fed by a feeding tube, and later by the nurses.

The therapists began early in the morning, with a series of tests. From morning until late afternoon, this was to be my schedule for the next three weeks – speech, occupational, and physical therapies. The staff were all very nice. I even began to enjoy the therapy a little, as long as it got my mind off of the real implications of my situation. To start off, I was seated at a table and one of the therapists emptied a jar of pennies in front of me. She said "Pick them up." I instinctively reached out my left hand, since it was the only one that worked. She quickly, but gently slapped my hand and said "No, use your right hand." Just as I dreaded, I could not pick up even one penny. It was also extremely disturbing to me to have to re-learn the English language. I had not realized it, but I had been speaking "Stroke-Language." It was almost as dismaying, to say the least, as finding out that my right hand was not fully functional. Everyone assured me, however, that I was making great progress.

After the first week, we drove to Topeka for my first brief visit to a familiar place. My home seemed welcoming, but unfamiliar and strange in the way that places do when you've been gone. Still, I relished the time. When we returned to Nebraska, one of the more bizarre events of my ordeal took place. Since I was now on out-patient status, we were staying in a local hotel. I was about to go to sleep when suddenly my thoughts turned to the Bible. There was a Gideon Bible on the nightstand next to the bed. I picked it up, and I was nearly frantic when I realized that I could not think of a single verse, nor any of its content. I could think of none of the names of the Sixty-six books, no names of Bible characters, none of the sto-

101

ries, nothing! I was nearly in panic when I asked Vicci to grab the Bible and read something to me – anything. With a puzzled look, she opened the Bible and began to read from John Chapter 6, the story of Jesus feeding the 5000. After thirty years of personal Bible study, and teaching adult classes, I was now hearing it for the first time! It was such a strange sensation. There was a faint air of familiarity about this story she was reading, and yet it was all new. What a peculiar thing, that a stroke can destroy a portion of the brain, and be that selective. I had panicked, because I instinctively knew how important it was. This Jesus I was hearing about was soothing, and I was eventually able to go to sleep. (Fortunately as of this writing, my Bible knowledge has returned.)

I returned to the clinic for two more weeks, and continued to improve and grow stronger. One day I discovered that there was a Piano in an open room on the second floor. I had not been thinking much about one of my greatest fears – not being able to make music. I sat down at the Piano, my right arm in my lap, and played a few figures and scales with my left hand. Then came the great test. I lifted my right arm and played a simple scale, although somewhat haltingly. I was surprised that I was even able to press the keys. However the real surprise happened when I tried to play with both hands. I found that I could play with right or left hand independently, but not with both hands simultaneously. I just could not do it. Initially I felt tremendously frustrated, and then fearful, but the Lord gave me a peace about it. I decided it would do no good to worry about it, and it would be best to leave my future in His hands. After working at it repeatedly, there was some progress. Katy was witness to this. She says "It was miraculous in that it's how your brain was remodeling in front of us. It shows rewiring and your tenacity to never give up."

After three weeks it was time to come home, and transfer to another Rehab Hospital in Topeka. I left Nebraska on a Friday, and was to enroll in the outpatient clinic in Topeka on the following Monday. I would be staying at home! The first night at home, I was awakened by a loud crashing, followed shortly by someone moaning. Startled awake, I lay there thinking I was dreaming. I got up and went to the bathroom, the same one in which I had the stroke, and I found Vicci lying in our sunken bathtub. I stared at her for a moment thinking "what in the world are you doing?" before I managed, with some difficulty, to get her back to bed. She had been disoriented from spending the previous night in a motel room, and stumbled and fell. I knew she was hurt, but I thought it was just bruises. The morning told a different story. Vicci could move, but only with great pain. My daughter Kate, who was staying with us, called 911. Here was I, partially disabled and unable to drive, and now my wife was facing a trial of her own. I began to feel a bit like Job in the Bible. The ambulance took her to the same hospital that I had been taken to, where we found out it was not bruises, but a fractured spine. After a painful night, she was scheduled for surgery the next day – with the same doctor, Dr. Allen, who had operated on me. Everyone was stunned that we were back in the hospital again, and this time for my wife. We sent out prayer requests – this time for Vicci.

They performed the surgery, a relatively new procedure called Vertebroplasty. They use a balloon and a type of cement to rebuild her vertebrae. There was no incision – it is done with a Laparoscope. After one more night in the Hospital, she was home, and feeling nearly normal. I couldn't believe she was back home after breaking her back. The doctor said that were it not for this type of surgery, she would have been *months* recovering. I thanked him for his work on her, and myself. I felt that we had narrowly escaped a calamity. Vicci's incident had fallen right on the day that I had an appointment to enroll in the Rehab program, so it was delayed, but I started it the following week. The clinic was similar to the one in Nebraska. They tested my hand for numbness, as well as a full battery of other tests. The various therapies continued – as did the improvements. I was basically aware that I was slowly getting better, but I really didn't grasp how much I was improving. People that I spoke to on an occasional basis always remarked about how much better I was speaking. The change was so gradual, that I could scarcely notice it. Over time, the feeling was coming back to my hand, at least partially. I finally sat down at my Piano, and suddenly I could play with both hands! It was nowhere near my former ability, but now I had hope. As the days have passed, my playing improves slowly – I can even play the Guitar! (Although I must use a thumb pick.)

There are some remaining speech problems, and I have trouble with Neuropathy in my right side. It has been a long and hard struggle, and there is still a ways to go. I did not know it at first, but this stroke was extremely serious. I just now am finding out how serious. My Doctor, after conferring with several other physicians including a hematologist, told me that they thought what had caused the stroke was a blood disorder called "antiphospholipid syndrome." He said that it was unlikely that a physical exam would have revealed it. It is a type of auto-immune disorder, and he informed me that I must be on blood-thinner drugs, presumably for the rest of my life. I was not pleased about having to take Coumadin (better known as Warfarin,) but I left his office resolved to take whatever medicine they recommended. More significant is what my Neurologist, Dr. Welch, told me. He had not seen me in many weeks, in fact since the days in the emergency room in the Hospital. When he walked into the room, I jumped to my feet, held out my hand, and said "Hi, Doc!" It would be hard to miss the look of astonishment on his face. He was clearly pleased with my progress, but then he told me "Mr. Livgren, you had as bad a stroke as a man can have." He said "Once in a while, a Doctor gets to see someone like you." I had been getting comments like this all along, but I was just now starting to get it. Clearly, something was going on. I should, by all rights, be either deceased, or confined to a wheelchair, yet I am not seriously disabled. The comment was made that I was "like Job," yet Job received back all that he lost and more besides.

I have come to believe that my Father in Heaven has once again shown us His kind mercies. I have many times been the recipient of His mercies before, as when He saved Vicci from her head injury in 1998. Now, He has saved me. He exists, and he hears the prayers of His people. I know I am nothing special. I know that sometimes there are good, prayerful people whose prayers are not answered, for which I have no explanation. He is the Lord God and mercy is His to give, and He gave it. Throughout this whole ordeal, I somehow knew that it was going to be alright. I felt a kind of calming presence, the presence of Christ, telling me that I need not fear. I pray that I be fully recovered, but if not, then whatever the Lord gives me is enough.

Addendum

In May of 2011 I was contacted by Stormont Vail Hospital, and was invited to attend a "Stroke Conference" that they were hosting. Many Doctors and Nurses, and well as people from Kansas Rehab Hospital would be attending. Dr. Allen, who had done my Surgical procedure, would be one of the featured speakers. It would be held at the Pozez Education Center Auditorium in Topeka. The star of this show was to be, you guessed it – me. Vicci and I were seated among all the Doctors and Nurses. As we began listening to Dr. Allen make his presentation, the lights dimmed and a Movie screen was lowered. He showed the audience several charts and graphs which had all sorts of Medical information. The terminology was way over my head, but I understood the essential message – I had been in a *very* precarious state.

Then came the coup de grâce. Suddenly a very large color 3D image of a skull appeared on the screen. It was slowly rotating, while alternating on the horizontal and vertical axis. Dr. Allen said "This is the image taken of Mr. Livgren's...." That's as far as I got. His words all became blurred. I was stunned. No man should have to see an image of his own skull. Ever since I was a little kid I have not liked skulls. To me, they represent death. Instinctively, I turned my head away, but curiosity got the best of me. I looked at it again, timidly. Now I was transfixed on this image. As I recovered my senses, I began to hear what the Doctor was saying. "As you know, Yellow represents healthy brain tissue, Red is tissue in jeopardy, and Blue is tissue that is dead, and unrecoverable. As you can see, the right half of Mr. Livgren's brain was Blue." I was even more stunned. No one had told us this before, especially in such graphic terms. Then Dr. Allen said "Now look at this image, taken later. As you can see, except for this very small area of Blue, the right half is all Yellow."

I sat in my seat, unable to move. Did I hear that correctly? I turned and looked at Vicci, and the look on her face confirmed it. My brain had been "resurrected." As I grappled with this fact, I was lost to the Conference. More blurred words. It probably was all Medical Terminology that I would not have comprehended any-way. But I snapped out of it as Dr. Allen proceeded to give his the-ory of what had happened. He told the audience that he thought that somehow my body had known beforehand that this stroke was going to occur, and that I had grown "auxiliary blood vessels" to supply my brain with oxygen. I remember thinking that this sce-nario would be more miraculous than the fact that my brain had simply been resurrected. As I was pondering this, I heard a voice summoning me to the stage. There was applause. I got up from my seat, and went to the Podium. I was nearly speechless. I had been very much looking forward to showing everyone how well I was doing, but my mind was filled with that rotating skull, and Blue brain. It couldn't have been much of a speech. More applause, and it was over.

The crowd was leaving the Auditorium as I walked up the aisle to Dr. Allen. After making some small talk, I said "Dr. Allen, do you really believe your theory? Do you really think that's what hap-pened?" He just smiled and said "Not really."

The Early Gigs

It's time to dust off the history books of my memory. I cannot possibly remember every concert that Kansas played when we first started touring. There were so many, but there are four which stand out to me. The first was at a club in Manhattan, Kansas called "Canterbury Court." We had just (thankfully) changed our name from "White Clover" to "Kansas." I had been playing with the second version of Kansas prior to joining up with White Clover. The remaining members of Kansas decided to hang it up, so we took the name once again. Besides, the name "White Clover" sounded a bit too much like a band from the "Flower Power" era. "Kansas" was timeless. The band was just beginning to get our sound together. The songwriting of Steve Walsh and myself was starting to take shape, and the musicianship of the players was getting tight and powerful. In short, we were beginning to get some local notoriety and were ready to "blow another act off the stage." We were very excited about this gig. It was, in fact, the first time that Kansas was to open the show for a well known Recording Band. It was "Bloodrock." They were a Texas band that had come on the scene in 1971 with their semi-hit song "D.O.A." Since that time they had gone through some personnel changes, so we really didn't know what to expect.

It was cramped quarters, but we set up our equipment in front of them. We were primed and ready, and our debut as an opening act went extremely well. It was almost as if the audience could sense that we were on the brink of fame and fortune, and they went crazy for us. Bloodrock was quite good, but on this night they couldn't really compete with the "local boys." What was particularly interesting about them to me was their Lead Vocalist, a guy named Warren Ham. Not only could he sing, but his voice was unique. Plus, he could play multiple instruments including Flute, Sax, and Keyboards. I immediately put him on my "Musicians of Interest" list. (As many of you know, several years later Warren was featured in my band "A.D." as well as some of my solo work.) Warren has since been a sideman for many major artists, and is currently a member of Ringo Starr's band. In addition, he became a good friend.

Kansas was not actually touring yet – we had been an opening act for another band that *was* touring. One day in April of 1974, while waiting for our first album to be released, we received a phone call from our management. We were to load up our equipment (in our new Anvil Cases which had just arrived) and drive to Lincoln, Nebraska to open the show for the "J. Geils Band." Man, were we excited as we pulled up to the Concert Hall. This would be the second "professional concert" that we were to play. We were familiar with the J. Geils Band, but we were not exactly fans. They just weren't our "cup of tea."

We had just got our gear unloaded. We were still doing that ourselves, with the assistance of Jerry Gilleland, our Roadie. The Stage manager walked up and said "Your Dressing Room is over here." We just stood there, unable to process what he had just said. We had never had our own "Dressing Room" before. The hundreds of Clubs that we had played never really had a proper Dressing Room. We walked into the room. There it was, with mirrors, "make-up" lighting, and racks to hang our clothes on. There was one more thing. A large round tray heaped up with all sorts of Cold Cuts, Lettuce, Pickles, Olives, and so on. There were jars of Mustard, Mayonnaise, and Ketchup. There were loaves of Bread, White and Wheat. There was a tub full of crushed ice with all sorts of Beverages. To top it all off, there was a bottle of Bourbon, and a bottle of Vodka (the expensive kind!) We looked at each other, feeling a bit bewildered. Somebody said to Jerry "We're in the wrong Dressing Room. Go find out where we're supposed to be." Jerry left us standing there, and shortly reappeared. "No," he said. "This is the right room. That stuff is for you guys." Now we were *really* bewildered! These cold cuts were for *us*? Someone bought us all this food? It is said by some that "The way to a man's heart is through his stomach." In the case of the members of Kansas, that statement is exactly true. There was not a shred of Baloney, a

Pickle, or even a single Olive left when we got through with that tray. What a cool Promoter to do this for us! Of course, we were ignorant of the fact that *all* Promoters furnish some sort of food and drinks for the artists. We soon found out that the food tray we got that night was actually quite modest, but for us it was a Gourmet feast! We played well that night, on the biggest stage we had yet been on. We watched the J. Geils Band intently from the side of the stage. We were very interested, not so much in their music, but in their showmanship. They really knew how to "work an audience." We took "mental" notes. Back in Topeka again, we settled into our routine of waiting for our album to be released. This was a frustrating period for the band. We had been in New York City to record the album, at the famous Record Plant studio no less, and here we were twiddling our thumbs in Topeka. People were beginning to wonder if we had invented this big story about going to New York and recording an album.

Things were starting to happen, however. Just in time we heard about another promising concert date. We had played the night before at a club in Galena, Kansas. It was a rough "beer bar" kind of place – the kind of gig that bands have to play to survive. We had to pull out our "cover" songs. Little did we know this would be the last time we had to do that. The next night, April 22, 1974, we were to play at the famous Cowtown Ball Room in Kansas City. This was one of our "dream gigs." The Cowtown was one of the legendary concert venues in the Midwest. I had been there many times, attending performances by some of my favorite bands. I had seen Frank Zappa, King Crimson, and Gentle Giant there. And now we get to perform on that stage! The funny part was, we were opening for Captain Beefheart. He was, shall we say, an extremely interesting musical artist. I use the term "artist" quite literally. There was no one like him, or even close. I remember listening to, and laughing hysterically to his "Trout Mask Replica" album in 1970. Again, it was not a perfect match-up with Kansas, but we certainly took the gig. For that matter, we would have opened for "Tiny Tim" if it meant playing at the Cowtown Ballroom.

The concert went extremely well, except for one thing. The night before, Steve Walsh began to get really sick. (I will not reveal the nature of his ailment.) Merle McClain, our lighting technician, and I heard Steve moaning in the adjacent room. It was the middle of the night, but we rushed him to a local Emergency Room. Good thing we did. The Medic took one look and knew what the problem was. They prescribed some medication, and told him to take it easy for a while. We said nothing about the concert we were to play that evening – one of the biggest bookings we had ever had. Steve was in excruciating pain that night. Barely able to sit on the bench of his Hammond B3, he nonetheless sang and played flawlessly, if not a little less enthusiastically. The crowd loved us. Captain Beefheart was just what I expected – Captain Beefheart. He could be no less. In later years I became somewhat of a fan of his, if for no other reason than for his total originality.

Once more we were in Topeka, waiting, and still waiting. It nearly drove us to distraction. Relief came once again with a phone call. This was much more than a gig – it was news of our first tour! The opening show was to be in Phoenix, Arizona, and we were booked to play concerts in several cities with the Kinks. The Kinks! How ironic that this tour would consist of opening the show for one of my favorite bands of the early Sixties. The Kinks, along with the Yardbirds, were at the top of my "most admired" list. This was going to be magnificent! Playing with the Kinks! We actually rented our first car to make the trip – a big Chevy Station Wagon. We piled into it, along with what passed for our luggage. The drive to Phoenix was exciting for us because it was unknown territory, but more so because we could sense that this was the beginning of our career as touring musicians.

On May 9th 1974, we pulled up at the Celebrity Theater in Phoenix. As we unloaded our gear, we couldn't help but notice that this venue was unlike any we had seen. The stage was in the center of the room, and was completely surrounded by the audience. It was circular. Jerry told us that it rotated. Wow! As usual, we were cramped on stage. Kansas was just not cut out to be an opening act.

We had six members of the band, and I had both a guitar setup and a keyboard rig. Nevertheless, we were prepared to "do battle." For the next two years (at least,) this would be the fate of Kansas – to be the opening act for some other band. Once again, we had a Dressing Room, with the accompanying Baloney and Bread, for which we were thankful. It was consumed. When it came time to play, we were ushered down to the stage. As we started our first song, I felt a mild jolt, and the stage started rotating. It was the weirdest sensation. I couldn't relate to the audience. Just when I got used to seeing a face, it became a different person the next time I looked up. Peculiar. Our performance was a little over excited, but it went well. When we finished our last song, we were told to exit the left side of the stage, which was lined up with our Dressing Room. We got to the room, all excited and out of breath. We had played our first date on a tour! Then somebody said "Hey, where's Rich?" Nobody knew. Rich was missing. We walked down the hall and opened the stage door. The house lights were on. There, in the middle of the audience, with his guitar still on, was Rich. Rich was a very big guy, and he was struggling between the narrow aisles saying "Excuse me, excuse me." People were trying to get out of his way, and direct him to the Dressing Room, which was on the opposite side of the hall. Rich had obviously not heard the message about exiting the stage to the left. The members of the band still laugh, including Rich, every time we are reminded of this story.

The Kinks. We were all watching. As they took the stage, with lights dimmed, the announcer said "Ladies and Gentlemen, please welcome the Kinks!" There they were, one of the idols of my youth. I never dreamed I would ever get to see them, much less play with them. They played their first number, but during their second song, something was clearly wrong. The two brothers, Ray and Dave Davies, were scowling at one another. They weren't joking. Suddenly, one of them picked up a pitcher of beer (where that came from is anybody's guess,) and poured it over his brothers head. Then they erupted in a "knock down" fist fight. Roadies and managers stormed the stage. The house lights came on, and the concert seemed to be over – after two songs. So much for the

Kinks. After a while they came back on stage and finished the show as if nothing unusual had happened. Apparently, par for the course. We went on to California to play several more shows with them, before starting up on a tour with Mott the Hoople. Every concert was an education. We were learning how to play and act like a professional touring band. It was about time.

The Acquisition of 2880

In the early 1950's, when I was just a toddler, we lived in a tiny
one-room bungalow right next to my Grandparent's house. Actually, I think it was a converted garage, known as a "Garlow." This
was the famed "Polka-Dotted house" on Kansas Avenue. I swear, it
really was painted in Polka-Dots. I believe it is still in existence,
though someone has obviously painted it in a more conventional
way.

My Dad had just acquired a new job at the Goodyear Plant, and being in need of family space, began to look for prospective building
sites. He found a lot on what was then the South edge of town, and
took what savings our family had managed to accumulate and
bought it. I remember it as nothing more than a grassy mound, but
it was ours! From that location, one could survey the surrounding
hillsides and pastures. Our address was 2830 Sunset Drive. Well
named, because from there you could easily see every Sunset.
There were very few houses in the area back then. Being on a very
modest budget, my Dad began framing the house with my Grandpa
Charlie, who was a carpenter by trade. At this rural address, there
was no power yet, so it was built using only hand tools. No electric
saws, no Nail-guns, it was hand-built.

It was nothing spectacular to look at. Just a rectangular-box
dwelling place, but I was fascinated watching it take shape as Dad
and Grandpa hammered and sawed. My Dad, to me, was a wonder-
worker who knew everything that could be known, and knew how
to accomplish it. I don't really remember much about living in the
Polka-Dotted house, I was too young, but I am filled with memories of our new house. My childhood through my teen years all
took place there. I can recall every square inch of that house, the
yard, the neighbor's yards, and the surrounding acreages. I played
My Dad's old piano in the basement there, and picked my first
notes on a Guitar in the living room. I wrote my first song there,

and formed my first band, the Gimlets. It was "Ground Zero" for much of my life. After we had lived there for a few blissful years, we received a notice from the City of Topeka. We were being annexed. I didn't know exactly what "annexed" meant, but by the look on my Mother's face it was not good. "Our address is no longer 2830 Sunset Drive" she said. "It's 2880 Mulvane." She sounded so broken-hearted. *Mulvane* ? Yuck! A long way from Sunset Drive. Anyway, we were officially Topekans now and we soon got used to it. Along with the address change, our neighborhood was beginning to change with unprecedented home-building. We were living in Suburbia.

The bliss of this Suburban life continued. The years flew by, and I grew up. My memories of what took place in that house are rich and plentiful. But as is nearly always the case, it had to come to an end. In my twentieth year, my Dad was informed by Goodyear that he was being promoted. That was a good thing, but along with it came some shattering news. He was to move to Akron, Ohio. My family didn't know what to make of it. In my wildest imaginings, a move was never part of it. We had lived here our whole lives, and we couldn't conceive of living anywhere else. My Dad held a big family "Pow-Wow" to help him decide what to do. In his heart, I think he already knew, but for our sake we had to talk it over. My Mom was adamant about staying, but she was the picture of a submissive wife and said she would do whatever Dad felt was best. We kids were all against it. *Ohio?* We had never even been there, and had no interest in going there. We all cried, but Dad held sway. We were moving. For myself, the decision was even more traumatic. It was not just the move, but whether or not I was going with my family, or striking out on my own. I was nearly 20 years old, and it was getting to be high time for independence. I decided to stay in Topeka with my friends, and try to make a living playing music. This really broke my parent's hearts. Not only were they going to lose our beloved home, but their number one son as well. The fact that I was going to be a Musician made it even worse. When the day came, many tears were shed by everyone. No one knew what this separation was going to be like. We said our goodbyes, and got on with our lives. (As it turned out, they were only there a few years before Goodyear moved them back to Topeka! 2880 Mulvane, however, was occupied by another family.)

Fast forward to the Winter of 2013. Myself, Vicci, and the kids were now living on a farm in Berryton, Kansas, very near to Topeka. We had been there since 1993, after we moved back from Georgia. Literally, the day we got back to Kansas, I had to cruise past my old home. There it was, looking just like I remembered it. This became a ritual when I was in the neighborhood, and every Christmas season we would drive by and see the houses all lit up. I always looked for, (and silently hoped for,) a "For Sale" sign to appear on the property, but to no avail. Someone was obviously living there, but I never bothered them. Perhaps it was needless for me to think this way, but I figured the last thing they needed was some starry-eyed visitor telling them the history of the house and all the tall tales of my youth.

One day, my brother Cal was in town for some work, (he lives in Springfield, Missouri,) and he decided to drive past the old place and reminisce. As he pulled up, he noticed that someone appeared to be moving out. There was furniture on the lawn. Cal quickly jumped out of his truck, walked up to the man in the driveway, and asked "Is somebody moving out?" "Yes", he said, "but we haven't even listed it yet." "Wait just a minute" Cal said. "I might just have a buyer for you." Cal immediately called me on his Cell Phone. When I picked up my phone I was pleased to hear the voice of my little brother. I started to chat, but he quickly interrupted and said "Kerry, 2880 is for sale!" Silence. "Say that again, Cal, just so I understand." "2880 is for sale." "Catch you later." I blurted out, and hung up. At lightning speed I called a Real Estate agent I knew from Church, Connie Davidson, and told her what I had just heard. I'm sure she could tell by the excited tone of my voice that I was pretty serious. "Connie, check on a listing on 2880 Mulvane! I very much want to buy it! Call me back as soon as possible! I want to buy it!" She must have thought I was nuts. Reality had not yet sunk in. I had not even given a thought to how I was going to pay for it, or what I was going to do with it. I only knew I wanted it. Usually, with an expenditure of this magnitude, I would spend some time thinking over all the ramifications of the purchase, and pray about it before making a move. Not this time. My impulse acted before my brain could even get in gear. I paced back and forth on the floor for about half an hour before my phone rang. I looked at the phone, and the screen said "Connie Davidson." I took a deep breath, and pressed the button. "Kerry, there is no multiple listing yet, but I got the name of the seller. We can make an offer if you want." "Yes, YES, I want!" I could hardly contain my excitement.

Over the next couple of days there was some going back and forth on the price, but I can say we arrived at a very satisfactory conclusion. I am the proud owner of the house of my childhood! Now comes the big payoff – I get to enter the house. As we pulled into the driveway, it felt like I was in a cloud, or some sort of fantasy. We opened the front door. I was almost scared to walk inside. As I stepped in the door, I was swimming in memories. It was the same house I remembered, yet something was different. The years had taken a toll, and there were some modifications the owner's had made, yet the shell of the house was still the same. I walked through the living room to the South end. There it was, my old bedroom. My head was in a fog – this all seemed so unreal. One of my initial impressions involved the size of the dwelling. The entire house seemed much smaller than I remembered it. I have since talked to a number of people who, in similar circumstances, experienced the same thing. But I swear, it's smaller. Small or not, it's an incredible blessing to own this house. Few people, I suppose, get the chance to re-acquire the home of their youth. The yard where I flew kites and balsa wood gliders, the kitchen where my Mom cooked our breakfast every morning before School, the basement and the garage where the "Gimlets" got together and rehearsed. I could go on and on. And of course the fact that my brother "just happened" to be driving by – it's all too much. So what has been the result of owning this house? Well, for one thing, we acquired it just as my son, Kyle, was getting out of the Navy. I asked him if he was interested in living in "the house that Grandpa built," and he said "Sure, Dad, are you kidding?" He lived there for several years before we began renting it out. Was it worth it and would I do it again? The answer is a resounding yes! Best buy ever. Although I will have to admit – it's been a bit of a "money pit." We've had to do quite a few expensive "modifications" of our own, but I regret not a penny. The only caveat I have for folks who are contemplating such a purchase is: You can never bring back your memories. Even though the things I remember all happened here, in this house and in this yard, they happened in a different moment of time. If you are expecting more you will be disappointed. But man, it's close!

Grandma Grape and the Robin

Most people have no memories of their Great Grandparents. By the time they are old enough to remember anything, their Great Grandparents are gone. I have one incident that I can remember, involving my Great Grandmother on my Mother's side of the family. (The Linville's) I was three years old at the time, and she was obviously quite advanced in years. I don't recall ever hearing her speak. She never uttered a word. Her habit was to sit on the front porch in a rocking chair, and observe me playing in the front yard. She was the very picture of anyone's Great Grandmother. To me, her name was "Grandma Grape." Being only three, I was not yet able to speak fluently, and that was my attempt to say "Grandma Great." The name stuck, and I never knew her by any other name.

Like any three year old, I was prone to acts of mischief. I would grab a handful of dust, creep up behind her, throw the dust at her and then run away. If my parents had witnessed this, I would have, (and should have) been thoroughly spanked. However, I repeatedly got away with it. Grandma Grape never seemed to react to my playful pranks. She would just calmly brush away the dust and continue rocking until I did it again. I never seemed to get a reaction from her.

One Spring day, however, she would get her revenge. There was a very large tree in the front yard, to which my Grandpa had fashioned a rope swing. I spent countless hours swinging back and forth on it. On this day Grandma Grape was on the porch as usual, and I was just sitting in my swing, dangling my feet. Suddenly, I felt something go "splat" on the top of my head. This was a new experience. It didn't exactly hurt, but it somehow felt very unpleasant, and unnatural. I instinctively looked up, and there, perched on a branch directly above me, was a Robin. He had expelled his load of waste directly on my head. I had been "bird-bombed!" Out of pure humiliation, I began to cry, and I ran to Grandma Grape for comfort. From her vantage point, she had seen the whole thing take place. It was the only time I saw her react – with laughter. She could hardly contain herself. There was justice in the world! All those shenanigans I had inflicted on her had been atoned for.

My Mother heard me squalling on the porch, and came out of the house to see what the commotion was. She found me, with my "baptism" on my head, and Grandma Grape in a paroxysm of mirth. My discomfort had inadvertently provided my Grandma Grape with a moment of entertainment. I never threw dust at her again. I can still hear the laughter.

A Broken Arm and Yardbirds in Emporia

In December 1965, I was a Sophomore at Topeka West High
School. I had only been there a couple of months, and like any
"newbie," adjusting to High School was a bit traumatic. To complicate things, my right arm was not fully functional. I couldn't extend
my elbow. The previous Spring, the evening before I was to graduate from Jardine Junior High School, I had been racing bicycles
down Mulvane street with my friend, Danny Slack. The problem
arose with a misunderstanding. (They always do!) Danny, who was
riding on my left side, thought that we were racing to the entrance
of our driveway on my right. I, on the other hand, was racing
straight ahead to the end of the block. At full speed, we arrived at
the driveway. Danny was a bit ahead, and being pre-progammed to
do so, he turned in front of me. Slow motion. I slammed into the
side of his bike, and immediately went airborne. I landed with all
of my weight, directly on my right elbow, then tumbled on the hard
pavement. I lay there for a couple of seconds, assessing the damage. I thought perhaps I was all right, just scratched up. Light
headed, I rose to my feet. I remember thinking that my right arm
felt really funny. I looked down and saw blood, spurting rhythmi-
cally from my arm. When I tried to extend my arm, it just "kept
going" until it was hanging straight down. My elbow was bent
completely backwards. There was something else. An object which
was gleaming white was protruding from my elbow joint.

The next thing I can remember is my Mother's face over me, and
the sound of a siren. I had no idea how long I had been out. They
loaded me into the Ambulance, and then I blacked out again. I
came to in the Hospital, with a new companion – pain. I had never
felt pain like that, and it seemed to be getting progressively worse.
By this time, I was in shock. This was a Friday night, arguably the
worst time to take a trip to the Emergency Room. It was the Weekend, and I needed a Bone Surgeon immediately. There was not one
available, plus, I really needed something for this pain. My Mother

was pleading with an orderly to get me some relief. I passed out again. After this, it was (mercifully) just a blur. I remember slowly emerging from an unconscious state. There was a Doctor I did not know bending over me, and I could see several members of my family in this Hospital Room. Mom and Dad were there, along with my Grandpa Jewell and My Great Aunt Lily. "Kerry, this is Doctor Gendel. He fixed your arm." my Mom said. Doctor Gendel then began explaining to everyone in the room the necessity of my remaining motionless. My right arm was held in an arc above my head, suspended by some sort of complex apparatus. There was a metal pin through my elbow, protruding from either side. Listening to him talking about all the details of my shattered bone, I began to feel sick to my stomach. "How long do I have to be here? I asked. He looked at me with sympathetic eyes. "Most likely, it will be about six weeks, young man. You had a compound fracture, and we had to rebuild your elbow. It will take that long for it to heal." This was a nightmare. *Six Weeks*? Oh, no! Surely I heard him wrong. The thought of having to spend six weeks in bed, with nothing to do, was absolutely abhorrent. This was just the beginning of my summer vacation. "You can't do this to me!" I thought. "I've got plans!"

Well, all of my plans went on hold. There was nothing I could do except lie there. Overall, I can remember little about the six weeks I spent in a room at the St. Francis Hospital. I must have looked ridiculous with my arm up over my head. Sleeping was torture, but I got somewhat used to the routine. Bedpans were, well, no comment necessary. Nuns bathed me with wet cloths. I watched endless TV, from morning until bedtime. My Parents were there during visiting hours whenever they were able, but that was the only activity. One thing I do remember. Hunger. I was, for some reason, ravenous. I consumed the Hospital rations three times a day, but that just didn't do it. I complained to my Parents about being hungry all the time. "Honey, there is nothing we can do about it. They won't let me bring any food into your room." Mom said. I found out, however, that she was not that easily dissuaded.

My room was on the ground floor, and my bed was next to a window. One day, I heard tapping. I looked over, and there was Mom's beaming face. She tapped on the window and said "Can you open it?" With my left arm, I could just reach the sash of the window. I stretched over as far as I could and opened it. She glanced around, to see if anyone was looking, and handed me a warm plate covered with a Kitchen towel. I set it on my lap, and lifted the towel. A waft of delicious smelling steam rose up. "Spaghetti!" There was a heaping portion of home-cooked Spaghetti, complete with buttered Garlic Bread. There was even a cloth napkin and one of our forks from home. "Eat it fast." said Mom. I was only too happy to comply. With my tummy full of Pasta, I slipped the plate back out of the window. Mom smiled and glanced around to make sure of her stealth, then slipped away. This procedure was to be repeated several more times during my stay. What a Mom.

When the six weeks had passed, the day came for my release. Dr. Gendel and a couple of Nurses slowly helped me to sit upright. I was a bit dizzy, to put it mildly. Then they freed my arm from the apparatus which held it up. I was excited, but a little nervous. The Doctor hooked what looked to me like an electric drill to the pin in my elbow, and out it came. It all happened so fast that I hardly had time to say "Ouch!" The most curious thing was that my arm was still in its position over my head. Though I had been freed, it would not move. It had been there so long that the muscles in my shoulder were atrophied. Then it was time for me to stand up. My Mom and Dad were in the room. Before the accident, I had to look up to see my Dad's face. As I stood next to the Hospital bed, I was eye to eye with him. I had grown a couple of inches in six weeks! We all got a laugh out of that. "It must have been Mom's Spaghetti." I thought.

The following weeks were consumed with Physical Therapy. My shoulder recovered pretty quickly, but my elbow was another matter. It wouldn't budge. The bones had been so shattered, that the joint was nearly immobile. My arm just hung at a ninety degree angle. Even the slightest movement was excruciating. Working with the Physical Therapist, I could not move my elbow more than a couple of degrees. She was a nice lady, but it was torture. In a follow-up appointment with Dr. Gendel, he told us that I may not be able to fully extend my elbow. This was the first time I had faced the possibility of being permanently maimed. He told me that it depended on me, and suggested I try things like carrying around a bucket of sand. I thought about all the things that I would not be able to do, especially playing my guitar. I was determined that my arm was going to be normal again. For the next several months I worked hard at Physical Therapy, including "carrying a bucket of sand." Ever so slowly, there was some improvement.

Now, back to December, 1965. One of my primary "Therapies" had become playing my guitar. I had recently acquired a shiny new Silvertone Electric Guitar from the Sears Catalog. It provided me with plenty of Physical, and Psychological Therapy. I couldn't get enough of it. I practiced every day, sometimes for hours, and the benefits to my elbow were noticeable. I could almost pass for normal. In 1965, I already had a large record collection, and I was well versed on the music scene. There were many kinds of music that I listened to, and many bands that I liked, but there were two that rose to the top – The Kinks, and the Yardbirds. The Yardbirds were my favorite. From the first time I heard them, they "pushed my button." I don't know exactly what it was about them that I liked so much. The guitar work, for one thing. But it was more than that. They were much more serious musicians than most of the "British Invasion" bands. They just grabbed me. I remember going to Katz Drug Store, a local "Pharmacy Superstore" to browse their Phonograph Record Department, which was quite large for the time. While thumbing through the albums, I found the Yardbirds *Having a Rave Up* LP, a definite buy. I already had their previous album, *For Your Love,* which I had played the grooves off. I was ready to hear this new one. I just knew these guys were going to do something cool. I took it home, put it on our family's big stereo record player, and prepared to be blown away. I was not to be disappointed. The opening song was *Mister, You're a Better Man Than I.* I was stunned. Not only was the song well written, sung, and played, but that *Guitar Solo*! I had to play it again and again. Man, how did Jeff Beck do that? He had a really cool, fuzzy, pre-psychedelic guitar tone, and he knew how to bend a string. To this day, it remains one of my favorite guitar performances. There are many "covers" of this song, but nobody can capture it like Jeff Beck did.

One day in December, I got a phone call from a friend of mine, Karl Geiss. Karl could hardly catch his breath. "Kerry, you're not going to believe this! The Yardbirds are playing tonight in Emporia!" The group of friends that I hung out with were always playing tricks on one another. That was clearly the case here. Emporia, Kansas was a small town about 50 miles Southwest of Topeka. There was no way the Yardbirds could, or would be, performing there. "No, Kerry, I'm serious! I saw it in the paper!. They're playing at Renfro's!" Now, I knew it was a joke. Renfro's was a run down beer-joint. I had (illegally) played there a couple of times with "the Gimlets." "Come on, Karl, give it up." I said. "I'm coming over to your house right now." he said. "I'll prove it to you." A few minutes later, he was there. He had walked, or rather ran, and he was out of breath. "Look at this!" He shoved a small piece of paper at me. It was a clipping from a newspaper. The headline was "Famed Yardbirds Will Perform Here." My mouth was hanging open, I'm sure. "Karl, we've got to go!" I don't remember how I talked my Dad into loaning us the 61' Plymouth to drive to Emporia, but he did. I grabbed the album cover of *Having a Rave Up,* and we left immediately. I knew right where Renfro's was, and in less than an hour we were there. I was astonished at the lack of cars in the parking lot. There was a Yardbirds poster tacked to the outside wall. (I should have grabbed it!) We paid the nominal fee at the door, and we were in. Karl and I just looked at each other. There was almost nobody there, and the band was supposed to start in 45 minutes.

We wandered up to the stage. I stared in wonder at the big Vox "Super Beatle" amps. There was a Fender Telecaster in a Guitar stand. "I wonder if that was the Guitar that Jeff Beck played that solo on?" I thought to myself. I still could not believe that we were going to see the real Yardbirds. The 45 minutes ticked away, with agonizing slowness. A few more people showed up, but that was it. Suddenly they walked out on stage. It was them. Keith Relf, Paul Samwell-Smith, Chris Dreja, Jim McCarty, and of course, Jeff Beck. I was situated *right in front* of Jeff Beck. They played less than an hour. I was completely enraptured. They played sort of a "Best Of" set list from both of their albums. I got to see Beck play the Guitar solo on *Mister, You're a Better Man Than I,* and then they ended the show with a very electric performance of *"The Train Kept A-Rollin'."* They laid me flat. I was exhausted as they played their last note. They got enthusiastic applause from the dozen-or-so members of the audience. As they put their instruments down and started to walk off stage, I took a deep breath and shouted "Mr. Beck, can I please have your autograph, sir?" He turned to look at me, then walked over. I handed him my album cover and a ball-point pen. He smiled. After gushing about how great I thought his band was, he signed it and said "Don't you want the others?" "Sure!" said I. They all signed it, and then they were gone.

I will not forget being privileged to have an (almost) personal concert by the Yardbirds. The only thing I have never been able to figure out – what were they doing in Emporia, Kansas? It was a miracle.

Schloss Kronberg

In March of 1978 Kansas toured Europe for the first time. This was tremendously exciting for us, since at that time we had not done any gigs outside the U.S. (except Canada.) The band members had never been to Europe, except for Phil Ehart and Robby Steinhardt. Unlike a U.S tour, our wives were coming with us. (Otherwise, they would never speak to us again!) Cheap Trick, who had opened many shows for us, was to go along as our opening act. The itinerary was interesting. We were to land in London. Then we had a couple of shows in Holland, one in Sweden, one in France, and about seven in Germany. Then we were to come back to England for one show in London. I remember thinking "Why don't we just call it our German Tour." Apparently, Kansas was quite popular in Deutschland.

There are many stories I could tell that happened on that tour, but one stands out in my memory. Our tour dates had been scheduled with several days off in between shows, so that we could be "tourists," and come home having seen more than just the inside of the Halls and Hotel rooms. In Frankfurt, Germany, our tour itinerary listed "Schloss Kronberg" as the Hotel we would be staying at. I remembered enough of my High School German class to know that "Schloss" meant "Castle." This was going to be interesting. We drove on to what appeared to be a very beautiful golf course. If it wasn't, it should have been. As our van pulled up at the entrance to the Hotel our mouths were agape. Surely we're not staying *here*! Kansas was used to staying at the likes of a Motel 6, or at best a Holiday Inn. This was something that you saw in a movie or a travel brochure. It really was a Castle. We grabbed our bags, and walked into the Lobby. Actually, it was more like a grandiose hall with a huge imposing fireplace. Exquisite antique furniture was all around, and oil paintings lined the walls. There were sculptures and stained glass windows. It was obvious that we were sur-

126

rounded by history, and a bit of wealth. We got checked in and were given keys to our rooms. Though I knew we were in a Hotel, I couldn't shake the feeling that we were in someone's house. The Porter led us through winding hallways to our room, which was very ornate and spacious, especially for a Hotel in Europe. I had never stayed in a Hotel room with a chandelier in it before.

Once Vicci and I were settled in, I had to explore a bit. I roamed the halls until I happened on a room that looked to be a Library. There were dusty old books, in German of course. It felt a bit eerie overall, not like a haunted house or anything, just slightly eerie, as if the walls wanted to tell us something. I wandered down to the big Lobby. There was no one there except for a very distinguished looking Gentleman, who was seated on a couch. He said hello to me, and we struck up a conversation. It soon became evident that this man knew a great deal about the Schloss, and that he was in fact one of the family members who owned the Hotel. He talked about the dowager Empress Victoria Friedrich, who built the Castle in 1893. She was the mother of Germany's last Emperor, Friedrich Wilhelm II. I felt very privileged to have met him. He wished me good night, and I went back up to the room. Despite the history lesson, I still could not shake off the eeriness of the place. There was probably no justification for it. I was just an American with no experience staying in Castles. Vicci was waiting for me in our room, a bit eagerly I might add. She had been waiting alone in the quiet. I was telling her all about my encounter, when there was a knock on our door. It was getting late, and we certainly weren't expecting anyone. I cracked open the door. It was Dagmar. She was the European girlfriend of Tom Petersson, who was the Bass player with Cheap Trick. I'm not sure, but I think Tom met her in Holland. Cheap Trick was not staying at Schloss Kronberg, so I was not sure how she ended up traveling with us. She was normally a very attractive young lady, but right now she looked terrified. "May I come in please?" she asked. "I am really frightened." "Certainly," I said. "Come in and tell us what's wrong." She appeared to be on the verge of tears. She began telling us that, after she checked into her room, she looked up and saw the portrait on the wall. "I noticed that wherever I moved in the room, the eyes were following me." I wanted to help calm her down, but it was all I could do to keep from laughing. This was a classic case of imagination taking over. After a while, we managed to calm her down enough to get her back in her room. My sympathies were with her, staying alone there with that portrait gazing at her. Personally, also having a vivid imagination, I was awfully glad I had Vicci with me!

Unfortunately, we had to get up pretty early in the morning. It was a travel day. It would have been nice to have had more time to explore. We grabbed our bags and headed for the Lobby. The plan was to get some breakfast somewhere down the road, probably at a truck stop. Vicci and I were the first to arrive downstairs. Since we had a few minutes to kill, we decided to have a look around the ground floor. We wandered down the hallway a bit, which led us to the entrance of what appeared to be a grand dining room. Suddenly, we were startled by an immaculately dressed man, who was clearly a Head Waiter. He waived his hand and said "Zis way please!" Then he said, with the most heartbroken look on his face, "So *many* people are missing!" (This would be a line that Vicci and I would always remember.) We peered into the dining room. The faces of half a dozen smiling waiters peered back at us. They held white towels over their arms. There were tables set with (real) silverware. There was a Buffet with everything you could imagine for Breakfast, including various delicious looking Pastries. There was a huge, very ornate, silver Coffee Decanter. There were no customers. "Livgren!!" I was snapped out of my reverie by the voice of our Tour Manager. "Come on, we have to get going!" I looked at the face of the Head Waiter, and stammered out a hurried apology. He looked completely crestfallen. We made a rapid exit through the Lobby and into our Van, and said goodbye to our Castle. What we didn't know, was that in Europe, Breakfast is always included with your room. Our ignorance was our loss. I have always hated waste, *any* form of waste. My Mother had always drilled that into our heads, especially about wasting food. If there was anything truly haunting about Schloss Kronberg, it was that spectacular Breakfast that we missed. It has haunted me for years. If you ever have a chance to visit Frankfurt, make sure you visit this utterly romantic Castle, Schloss Kronberg. And, make sure to stay for Breakfast!

The Goodyear Christmas Party

When I was growing up, there was a certain ritual that developed over the years at Christmas time. It usually began the day after Halloween, when my "Christmas Countdown" began. Thanksgiving passed, and I delighted in the feasting, but to me it was just a memorial to commemorate the approach of Christmas. As you can probably tell, I *loved* Christmas. Next came the yearly viewing of "The Wizard of Oz." I'm not sure of the timing of this event, but our local TV Station always showed it in the Fall. Though it had nothing to do with Christmas, somehow I made it part of the ritual. Then there was the first day of December, the Christmas month! From this time forward, there were all sorts of Christmas-themed cartoons and specials to be watched. Various adaptations of Dicken's "A Christmas Carol" were always my favorite. Then there was the last day of School and my class Party the day before School was out. The Christmas vacation meant freedom, and in those days it was extremely long, second only to the (eternal) Summer vacation.

On the off chance that we had snow during these days, the level of excitement went to "Eleven." Seeing the Christmas lights go up, and the decorations that the City of Topeka put on Kansas Avenue almost made the anticipation unbearable. What really did it for me, however, was the annual Goodyear Christmas Party. My Dad was an employee of the Goodyear Tire and Rubber Company. He started with the company as a Buyer, who purchased all sort of Industrial Equipment from all sorts of Vendors. We always got a lot of "perks" during the Christmas season – mostly stuff like Nuts and giant cans of Popcorn. We always got at least a dozen Fruitcakes. The Party was held on a Saturday morning at the Topeka Fairgrounds, in one of the Exhibit Halls. Our family would load up in our Nash and try to get there early. Dad was always already there. He had loaded up his Lowery Organ and Leslie the night before, and set it up in the center of the Hall. He was the "Star of the

Show." (Well, except for Santa Claus, who was always there!) Goodyear had procured the services of my Dad as their musical entertainment. He knew every one of the Christmas Carols, both Religious and secular – and I literally mean every one of them! He always preferred playing the old standard Christian Christmas songs. At this event, he was my hero. (Actually, on a lot of other occasions as well.) There he was, my Dad, perched atop a big riser, decorated with garlands of Holly and Ribbons, and playing the Organ for all to hear. He looked magnificent! I was a proud kid!

The climax of the Goodyear Christmas Party was the toy giveaway. These were not cheap toys. Goodyear actually spent some bucks on their employees kids. Hundreds of kids lined up, and were restrained by a plastic "fence." They would stand there, peering at the tables of toys and scoping out which one to go for. The barrier would be dropped when they could restrain them no longer. At that moment it was "The Oklahoma Land Rush." Hordes of juveniles trampled all over one another to get the toy that they picked out. I don't know how Goodyear did it, but no child was disappointed. If they didn't get their first choice, there was always a second. If that was taken, there was a third. After all these years, I cannot remember what I got for Christmas at that Party, but my memory of my Dad up on that pedestal is forever crystal clear!

Recollections of Dust

As Vicci walked by the door of my music room, she stuck her head in and said "Honey, you really should do something with that. It's so pretty." My wife rarely commented on my songs, especially when they were not finished. She was making a notable exception for this one. Obviously, in retrospect, she was right. I had given no serious thought to the song. In fact, I didn't even think of it as a "song." A couple of years earlier another guitarist (in Des Moines, Iowa) showed me how to "Travis pick" on acoustic guitar. Though I considered myself a competent guitarist, I did not apply that description of myself as an acoustic guitarist, only electric. I had always played an electric guitar, and had very limited experience on an acoustic. Rich Williams had always handled most of the acoustic guitar tracks with Kansas. To try to better myself on the acoustic, I came up with this little "finger exercise," using a chord progression that fit it nicely. I was apparently oblivious to just how pretty it was.

After Vicci had steadfastly continued to make similar comments, I began to give it a serious listen from a songwriter's perspective. Though I began to appreciate the potential song, it never entered my mind to present it to Kansas. For one thing, it had no melody or lyrics yet, and secondly, it just wasn't the right style for the band. Kansas had been rehearsing for our "Point of Know Return" album, and in fact we had quit submitting songs. We were in the last stages of tightening up our performances before we headed for the studio, and I wasn't sure how the guys would react to a strange little acoustic song.

Nevertheless, I went to work on it. Composing the melody came to me rather effortlessly. It just rolled forth and felt very natural. While listening to it, I became aware for the first time of its melancholy and haunting nature. I knew that I would have to write lyrics to match. As I write this today, having played what would become

"Dust in the Wind" thousands of times onstage, I am reminded of the dreamy, and somehow calming, feeling it conveys. I have always been acutely aware of the temporary nature of our existence; that life is fleeting and that eventually all things pass away. When I was nine years old, both of my Grandmothers, and our family's best friend all died suddenly the same week. Needless to say, this had a powerful effect on me, one that I have never quite recovered from. I am not one who is obsessed with death, nor do I dwell on it all the time. In fact, I *love* being alive. It is our most precious gift. I am mindful, however, of the short duration of it.

The lyrics came to me fast and furious. I don't remember what specifically inspired the subject matter, but I could scarcely write them down fast enough. I had been reading several books recently, any one of which that could have triggered the lyrics, including a book of American Indian poetry. Though my reading has always influenced my writing, I was not quoting any particular source. I was simply following my own thoughts. The world is profuse with books and writings that deal with man's mortality and the "all is vanity" theme, but none quite as profound and beautiful as the Book of Ecclesiastes in the Bible, which the lyrics to "Dust" emulate. Though I had not read Ecclesiastes recently, it was definitely present in my memory. It didn't take long to put the song together, lyrics and melody. I had a 4-track analog recorder in my music room, (I didn't have a studio yet), and I remember doubling the acoustic guitar on two tracks, and recording a rudimentary vocal on a third. The next day at rehearsal, (as I recall it was our last day), I came in and announced that I had one more song that they needed to hear. Since I had done the same thing with our previous album, "Leftoverture," and the song was "Carry On Wayward Son," the guys wisely decided to give it a listen. I set up my 4-track and apologetically proclaimed that they probably weren't going to like this song, and that in my opinion it was not right for Kansas. I pressed the "play" button.

I don't remember exactly what happened next, but needless to say, my opinion of the song was very wrong. Steve took to the melody immediately. Rich was intrigued with the guitar part. Robby was very positive, though there were no violin parts written yet. There were no drums or bass at all in the song, yet even Phil and Dave liked it. I remember Dave saying "Kerry, where has this been?" Given the band's reaction, I was pleasantly surprised. We learned the song in a hasty rehearsal and we were off to the studio in Bogalusa, La. We didn't record any tracks on "Dust" there however, because we moved to Woodland Studio in Nashville to finish the album. I composed the string arrangement in a hotel room there, and went immediately to the studio where Robby recorded the Violin and Viola parts, finishing the song.

Our new work was recorded and mixed, but I still didn't realize what we had done. "Dust in the Wind" was to become Kansas' biggest success; a Multi-Platinum hit that crossed all radio formats, would endure for decades, and be recorded by a host of other artists. Did I get lucky? I don't think so. It was meant to be. I'm much more of a believer in design than random happenstance, nor do I measure the value of a song only by its commercial success. "Dust in the Wind" has meant much more than that. There is something in the lyrics that is true, that has "struck a chord" in the hearts of millions of listeners. It's not just the melody, Steve's beautiful vocal, or the memorable guitar theme. I believe it is the presence of God's truth – the inevitability that our lives in this world, every last one of them, comes to an end.

If I could change but one thing, I would change the lyrics somehow to be more positive and hopeful. Having found that hope myself, in becoming a Christian, I have since written many songs that convey a much more optimistic view of the world. I doubt, however, that I could ever top the impact of "Dust in the Wind."

Barney

During what I consider to be the "Glory" days of Kansas, 1976-1980, we amassed many great stories to tell. This has to be one of my favorites. It was 1978. We had worked our way to the West Coast while touring our latest release, "Two for the Show," and we were scheduled to play two successive shows at the LA Forum. They were both sold out, as I recall. As we pulled up to the venue, we were shown the way to our dressing rooms. In the hallway, we were met by our Manager, Budd Carr. He was smiling. It was not unusual for him to smile (particularly at a sold-out Kansas concert), but there was something different about this smile. It was the way a Magician might smile before he reveals the rabbit under his hat.

As soon as we got settled in, Budd called us all together. He was still smiling. He led us down the hall towards another dressing room, where there was a very large and imposing bodyguard stationed at the door. "What's going on?" I wondered. Smiling a huge smile, Budd opened the door. Sitting there was a small, nervous-looking man, who was clearly from the generation that preceded us. "Gentlemen, meet Mr. Don Knotts." It was *Barney Fife*! As recognition slowly came over us, we shouted "Barney!" We couldn't help ourselves. It was a gut reaction from years of conditioning. The hours of watching him on "The Andy Griffith Show" were absolutely overwhelming. I am sure he was quite used to it. Any time an actor plays a role that has such continued exposure, he would have to be accustomed to such adulation. America knew, and still knows him as "Barney Fife."

Now it was *us* who were smiling. "Barney" was very gracious. He shook all our hands while we embarrassed him with our praises. He came equipped with several 8 X 10 glossy photos, and signed them for us. Then Budd said "Guys, Mr. Knotts has agreed to introduce the band tonight." It is an understatement to say that we were pleased. Who could imagine? Budd later explained to us that

135

Mr. Knotts was represented by the same agency that Budd worked for, thus clearing up the mystery as to why he was at our show. At our sound check, as I was thinking about the upcoming introduction, I suddenly got an idea. I set my synthesizer to make a "whistling" sound. Quickly, the band worked up the Theme to the Andy Griffith TV Show. When it was time for the show to begin, the lights were dimmed and we took up our positions on stage. Out came "Barney," lit up by a single spotlight.

As he walked across the stage, we began to play the Theme song. He looked a little startled for a second, but being a consummate professional, he went with it. He took the microphone and yelled "Hi Kids!" in that familiar and unmistakable voice. We fully expected the audience to go wild, but instead there was light applause. They seemed confused, as if they weren't sure what was going on. Could it be, that *they did not recognize him*? Perhaps the context was just too improbable. Barney Fife introducing Kansas? No way.

Well, it was really him, and he did introduce us. "May I introduce, one of my very favorite bands, Kansas!" he exclaimed, and then he exited the stage and he was gone. When I dwell on this, and the context becomes too improbable for me to believe, I just look at that signed Photograph. Yep, we were really introduced by Barney Fife, even if the audience didn't get it!

Kansas Meets "Jaws" in Miami

We had not seen the Movie. It didn't exist yet, although in the Spring of 1975 it was about to become real. Several of us had read Peter Benchley's book, however, and it was still fresh in our minds. It was impossible to read those pages, and not be gripped or haunted by the imagery of oceanic monsters. We were all thrilled to see a Miami date appear on our tour schedule, as we had never seen the city before. In fact, many of the band members had never even seen the Ocean. After all, we were from Kansas – as far from the Sea as you can get. I had been to Oregon as a toddler, and to the Gulf of Mexico as a young teen, but that was it for me. Needless to say, we were excited about it. Our plane touched down at the Miami Airport. It was an early flight the day before the gig, so we planned on plenty of "beach time." As we exited the plane, I could have sworn that I could smell the sea air. We picked up our bags, got in our rented cars and headed for the Hotel on our itinerary.

To our great disappointment, which, in fact, bordered on horror, we had been booked at a Hotel at the Airport. The *Airport!* In Miami? We wanted to be on the beach! Though we were not in the habit of changing our reservations, this time we made an exception. After a few frantic phone calls, Jeff Glixman, who functioned as both our Sound Engineer and Road Manager, was able to get us booked into one of the many Motels on Miami Beach. Salvation! We hurriedly checked in, opened our bags to find our swimming trunks, and were on the beach inside of five minutes. There was a Lifeguard there, who told us to have fun, but not to swim after dark because the Sharks start coming in. Oblivious, we looked at each other and took off. I hit the waves at a full run. After splashing around for a few minutes, Jeff and I found a couple of Surfboards which were furnished by the motel. We were a couple of Midwestern boys who obviously knew less than nothing about Surfing, apart from what we had seen on the "beach" movies, but we climbed on them and started paddling.

When we got about 30 yards or so from shore, we turned around and tried to catch a wave. Jeff was slightly ahead and to the left of me when we started to paddle our way forward. Suddenly I felt a strange sensation on my right arm. I looked at it, and saw a foreign substance which had wrapped itself completely around my arm. At first, I thought it was seaweed, but that was not to be. A split second later it felt like 40 big Hornets had landed on my arm and all stung me at once. I had never felt anything like it. Involuntarily, I started screaming bloody murder and flailing the water, trying to get the offending stuff off of me. Jeff turned and looked at me, and immediately took off so fast that it looked like he had a big outboard motor attached to his Surfboard. Thanks a lot! (Though I really couldn't blame him.)

Still screaming as the pain increased, I fell off the surfboard and began trying to swim. This became increasingly difficult, as now my right arm was barely functioning. It felt really "rubbery." Thank goodness, the Lifeguard launched into action. He met me just as I reached the shore, and helped me up on the beach. The guys in the band all ran down to see what had happened. The Lifeguard took one look, and knew what had transpired. "Don't worry," he said. "It's just a Man of War." I looked at my arm, and there was a long blue-ish tentacle which had enveloped it. Anxiously, I said "Can you get it off of me?" As he started to carefully pick the gooey tentacles off my arm, I said "What the heck is a Man of War?" "A Portuguese Man of War." he replied. "It's a type of Jellyfish. You're just lucky the main stinger didn't get you. These small ones are just to numb their prey." "It sure doesn't feel like numbness to me!" I was nearly passing out. My arm felt like it was on fire. He had finished removing the tentacles, when he pulled me aside where no one could hear. He said "Now listen up. I know this is going to sound strange, but I want you to go up to your room, and pee all over your arm. It will stop the stinging." I just stood there, with a blank look on my face. "Say that again? I don't think I heard you right." He slowly repeated his words. "I want you to go to your room, and pee on your arm. I'm not kidding. It will make you feel a lot better." Normally, I would have busted out laughing, but under these painful circumstances, I was game for anything. I would have jumped through hoops if it would stop this stinging! I checked his face one more time to make to make sure this wasn't some sort of twisted joke. He was serious. "OK." I said, cautiously. "I'll try it."

I arrived at the door to my room, and with my one good arm I fished the room key out of the pocket of my swimming trunks. Inside, I disrobed and stepped into the shower. As I stood there, I realized that I had no idea how to comply with the Lifeguard's instructions. How exactly does one pee on one's upper arm? Without going into the embarrassment of detail, let's just say I was able to carry it out. Almost instantly, sweet relief began to spread over my arm. Indeed, the furious stinging was slowly giving way to glorious numbness. Who could have known? I have read many times that urine does not help with a Jellyfish sting. But this Kansas boy takes exception. It may have been psychosomatic, but I don't care. As embarrassing a story as this is, it sure worked miraculously for me!

Phil Keaggy and the Little Les Paul

If you have never heard of Phil Keaggy, that is unfortunate. Phil is one of the premier Guitarists of our, or probably any, generation. He is almost without peer on Acoustic Guitar, but he can "rip" with the best of them on the Electric. He has an extraordinary sense of melody. He is also a great writer, plus he can sing. To sum it up, he's just a great musician. I first heard of him, sort of, in 1970. A friend of mine, Larry Baker, worked in a local music store in Topeka. He also played Guitar and Saxophone in the first version of "Kansas." I was in the store browsing around, when Larry said "Kerry, you've got to hear this band. They're called Glass Harp. Listen to this guitar player." I can remember being impressed with them, but not enough to shell out the (very hard earned) cash to buy the album. (Sorry Phil...)

Years later, I was to meet Phil. I recall getting a letter of encouragement from him when I first became a Christian, but our first actual meeting was at one of his shows in Atlanta. I was *very* impressed with him as a Guitarist, but even more so with the man. Vicci and I took the opportunity to invite him and his wife, Bernadette, to come stay at our house in Dunwoody, one of Atlanta's many suburbs. They accepted the offer. Phil and I got to know each other pretty swiftly, and left the ladies upstairs to converse while we retired to my studio. We were "talking guitars" while focusing on my collection. Phil's eyes landed on a particular Guitar in the corner. It was a miniature "gold top" Les Paul, not much bigger than a ukulele. He appeared to be very interested, if not enraptured with this "mini" guitar. "Where did you get that, Kerry?" he asked. I explained to him that it was a gift given to me by one of the Japanese Musical Instrument manufacturers. After we lost our equipment in a storm in the Pacific on the way to Japan, they had very graciously replaced our Guitars, Amps, and Keyboards with reasonable facsimiles of our original equipment. All except, the Little Les Paul. It was not a direct replacement for any guitar that I had, nor any that I had heard of. The workmanship on it was excellent, and it was quite playable, but it was just so *tiny*. I had always thought of it as a very interesting "novelty" guitar, but not one that anyone would think seriously about playing.

Phil, however, had a gleam in his eye as he said "May I play it?" I laughed, and said "Sure, Phil, you can play any guitar I've got!" I plugged it into an Amplifier, and handed the tiny Guitar to him. It was love at first sight. He began playing the little instrument in his inimitable style. He clearly was fascinated with it, and I was fascinated listening to what he could do with it. He kept on playing, lost in "Guitar world." At that moment, the Little Les Paul's fate was sealed. I knew that I had been given that tiny instrument for a reason. The idea popped into my head, and I spoke it. "Phil, it's yours." I said. "What? Kerry, no, I couldn't possibly..." I interrupted him. "I could never play it as well as you have just now, so I want you to have it, and I won't hear otherwise." I put it in its little case. Reluctantly, Phil left with it, thanking me profusely. He has been playing it for years now. The Little Les Paul has found its proper owner. So if you go to see Phil Keaggy, which I highly recommend, you just might see it!

Eenie

I was mean. Well, not really, but I certainly had an ornery streak when it came to my two younger brothers. Given the least opportunity, I would fool them somehow, or play tricks on them. The tricks varied from relatively insignificant, to very multifaceted and elaborate. At worst, they bordered on being dangerous, such as rolling my brother Cal in an old tractor tire, two blocks down a hill and through an intersection. If my Dad had seen that one, he would have been furious and I would have paid the price, but I never got caught. I was not totally without merit, always being the protector of my little sister Emalie. She was ten years younger than I, and I was frequently having to come to her rescue on those occasions when my brothers were harassing her. I was her "Knight in Shining Armor." Of course, this rivalry was all good natured – we were just typical siblings.

On one occasion, however, I pulled out all the stops. This was going to be one for the record books. I really can't remember how I came up with the idea, but I do remember every detail of how I proceeded with it. I painstakingly, and secretly, built two identical dummies. They were very Scarecrow-like in appearance. I hid them both in my bedroom closet until an opportune time. I searched my imagination to come up with a name for my creation, and named them "Eenie". They both shared the same name, since I planned on "deploying" them as one being.

The next Wednesday, known as "Bowling Night" was my big opportunity. My parents both went Bowling on Wednesday night, leaving my brothers in my care. They suspected nothing, although perhaps they should have. When they returned home they frequently heard tales of some sort of "shenanigan." On this night, I waited until my parents had left and my brothers were out of sight, and I very stealthily hid one of the "Eenies" in the basement, in a dark place behind the stairwell. Then I took Eenie number two and stood him up in our back yard. When I came back in the house, I said to my brothers "Hey Chris and Cal, come here." (I conjured up a facial expression of fear and alarm.) "You guys, I just saw something really weird! I thought I saw a stranger lurking around our Neighborhood. He was creepy looking." They both gave me a look that was a mixture of skepticism and a bit of uneasiness. I had tricked them before, so they would not be inclined to take anything their big brother said at face value. I let about 15 minutes go by in order to let that sink in, then I burst into the room and excitedly said "Guys! I just heard on the Radio that there is some sort of Creature sneaking around the Knollwood neighborhood! They said its name was Eenie, and he steals children and carries them away and they are never seen again! He especially likes little boys! I *knew* I had seen something weird a while ago." Now their eyes got big. If there had been a Hollywood Producer around, I would have received an Academy Awards Nomination for Best Actor. There was still some skepticism on my brothers' faces, but I also detected a trace of foreboding.

I told them to stay close to me, and I would protect them. I said, "We better turn all the lights off. Eenie will think no one's home and he might not get us." I went and got one of Dad's flashlights, with Chris and Cal now clinging to me. I began to peer into the darkness outside our front picture window. Minutes passed in silence. My brothers' eyes were huge. Then I exclaimed "What's that! I thought I saw something moving toward our front door!" I had them hooked. I said "Come on, we have to get in the basement. That's the safest place where Eenie won't look for us!" Illuminated flashlight in hand, I led them down the stairs. My siblings were definitely spooked – there was not an inch between us. "Let's get behind the stairs." I said. "Get in front of me so I can protect us from behind." They obeyed me without question.

Then came the moment I had been waiting for! In the darkness, I edged them closer to the Stairwell and the waiting "Eenie." They were standing directly in front of his looming figure. With great anticipation of success, I flashed the beam precisely on Eenie.

"EENIE!!" I screamed. "RUN! RUN!" Chris and Cal both let out a shriek. I turned and ran as fast as I could, with them one step behind, yelling crazily the whole way. We ran out the garage door, down the driveway, and into the yard on the North side of the house, and from there to the back yard. I purposely let them overtake me just as they both turned the corner, and they ran towards the waiting arms of the second Eenie. "EENIE!!!" I yelled. They both screamed in terror and ran full speed in opposite directions.

My prank was a complete success. I fell down, laughing hysterically. My brothers kept running for a while, until they realized that I had not been carried away by Eenie, but was consumed with uproarious laughter. "KERRY!" Chris yelled. "Cal, come back, it was a trick!" Now my brothers were chasing me around the yard, trying to pummel me with sticks and stones. Once their adrenaline calmed down, we went back in the house, where I explained to them all the details of the "Eenie" conspiracy. I showed them the two Eenies up close. Their fear had turned to anger, which gradually metamorphosed into a reluctant sense of admiration for their big brother. When my parents got home, my siblings cried and moaned about how Kerry had "scared us, and played a trick on us," but it was half-hearted. They were stifling laughter the whole time. To my amazement, I never got in trouble. My Mom and Dad were a bit displeased with me, but I think they were secretly in awe of their scheming son!

Laser UFO

When it came time to tour the "Audio Visions" album, the members of Kansas knew we had to do something spectacular to enhance our show. For the past several years we had been on the treadmill of competition with other big touring bands, always trying to "up the ante." We hired a Laser Company to put together a Special Effect for us, which featured an animated Laser sequence to be based on one of our songs. It was the usual Green Laser light. Not knowing anything about Lasers, we asked the Technicians why we couldn't have another color. We got a very technical answer which was way over our heads, something about "The only different colors that are practical is green or red," and "green Lasers look much brighter than red Lasers." Well, OK. They're the experts.

At the rehearsal, they set it up, and placed reflective mirrors all over the stage, and even at the back corners of the Hall. They put tape borders on the stage marking out where we could, and could not stand. We got a stern lecture on Laser safety, and the dangers of standing too close, or worse, getting hit with one. Personally, I took it seriously and had no intention of standing too close to one of the beams. The first time they switched it on, there was a chorus of "ooh's and ah's" from the band. The brilliant green beams formed a "cage" of light, surrounding the band. It looked *really* cool. Then they lit up the entire Concert Hall. The amazing thing was that the brilliance of the light did not diminish in the distance. It was as bright in the far reaches of the Hall as it was on the stage. Robby, being Robby, got really close to one of the luminous shafts, and very cautiously reached out and touched it with his finger. "Ouch!!" He just looked at me and smiled. Then came the show stopper. They had worked out their animation for the song "Icarus – Borne on Wings of Steel" from our "Masque" album. As we started playing, the image of a Winged Horse, made entirely of green light, appeared on the wall behind us. His wings flapped, and he galloped around the Hall. By today's standards, it may not seem like much, but in 1980 it was awesome. We were thrilled, and so were the audiences. As we toured the US, the only negative thing about it was the number of times we heard the Hall managers say "No Lasers tonight." Apparently, it was more than many of the Fire Marshals could handle. They just weren't used to having their Halls lit up with a Laser, no matter how many times the Technicians explained it to them.

There was one particular occurrence I remember, which had nothing to do with our tour. We were staying at a Hotel in Virginia Beach, right on the Ocean. We had a day off, and the Laser Technicians were taking the opportunity to repair their machine, which had been acting up. There were several of us out on the balcony of one of our rooms, where they had the Laser set up. "I think I've got it fixed." said the Tech. The Sun had just set. "Watch this!" he said, with a wry smile on his face. There was one solitary, puffy little cloud out over the Ocean. He aimed it carefully, and switched it on. The Laser hummed for a second, then shot out its beam. The cloud, which had to be at least a mile away, lit up like a giant green Christmas light. We couldn't believe how bright it was. It looked spectacular. We had a good laugh, then he shut it down. The next morning, as I was having breakfast, one of our crew walked up and said "Kerry, have you seen this?" He handed me a copy of a local newspaper. "Local Residents Report UFO" was the headline. The article went on to say what the various "witnesses" had seen. They reported a "disc-shaped" object, and they described its flight characteristics and speed, etc. Oh, the human imagination knows no bounds. If they only knew that what they had seen was a Rock Band playing with their new toy!

The last time I saw the Laser was several years later. I had taken my family to Stone Mountain, Georgia, where on Summer evenings they had a Show which featured Lasers and Fireworks. We laid our blankets on the ground, got out our picnic supper, and prepared ourselves for the evening's entertainment. As it grew dark, the Laser Show began. There it was – our Winged Horse. *Our* Winged horse, doing exactly the same moves as it did on our tour. I couldn't believe it. I stood up and began shouting, until Vicci said "Sit down! People are staring." It ruined my whole evening, until I thought about it. Free Enterprise. The Laser Company had to make their investment back somehow. At least I got to see it on Stone Mountain!

My Top

I debated whether or not to include this story. I hope you see both the humor of it, and its strangeness. It was Christmas Eve, 1965. Our family had gone over to my Uncle Ole's house, which was a long established family custom. I always thought it was a bit strange to open all your presents on Christmas Eve, but apparently my cousins didn't think so. They had always done it that way. But I thought we got the better deal – presents on Christmas Eve *and* Christmas Morning!

My, how Uncle Ole loved Christmas. I can still picture his smiling face as he played Christmas songs on his Lowery Organ. Their small house was consistently lit up with every known form of Christmas lights, almost to excess, and certainly more than the other houses on their street. But to top it all off, he mounted an arrangement of large electric Bullhorns which blasted Christmas Music all over the known Universe. The neighbors never complained. They knew Uncle Ole.

My cousin Larry Livgren was 10 years my senior. I always looked up to him – he could play the guitar! He even showed me how to play my first chord. It was a G major. My cousin Betty Jane was 5 years older than I, and Linda was a year younger. I was 16 years old. Like any 16 year-old, I was very proud to be 16, and *very* careful not to humiliate myself in any way before my cousins. To the teenage mind, that was always to be avoided. There were some other relatives or friends there that we saw at Christmas, but rarely beyond that. One such was my Great Aunt Lyda. She was not really my Aunt, except by marriage. Really, I hardly knew her, but she obviously knew me well enough, or thought she did, to merit her Christmas list.

After a big dinner of Holiday fare, the festivities began. Presents were opened beginning with the youngest first, so my little sister

Emalie and my two brothers, Chris and Cal, started it off. We started with the presents from Great Aunt Lyda, (Perhaps because they would be the least significant? Shame on us!) I watched eagerly as Chris and Cal opened their gifts. To my surprise, they were pretty cool! I don't remember now what they were, but I can recall thinking "Way to go, Aunt Lyda!" I was next. With great enthusiasm I began opening the box addressed to me. All eyes were on me. I removed the wrapping paper and opened the box. "What the... What's this?" It *must* be some kind of mistake. It was a Top. A toy Top. I was holding a Top in my hands, the kind of Top that my little brothers should get. I was 16. I began to hear snickering in the room. I could feel the beginnings of extreme humiliation welling up inside me. I heard my Mother's voice saying "Oh, how sweet! Kerry, tell Aunt Lyda thank you!" I could not speak. My brothers, being my brothers, were rolling on the floor in laughter at their big brother's ultimate indignity. I wrapped up the Top, and stowed it somewhere among the heaps of wrapping paper where I would never see it again. It was a Christmas I will never forget.

On through the years to the Spring of 2008. My Father had just passed away, and we had decided that My Mother was going to go live with my brother Cal in Springfield, Missouri. We were engaged in the sad and unpleasant task of sorting through their possessions. Their house in Warrensburg was a modest home, but it's amazing how much stuff people can accumulate in a lifetime. I was in the Garage, sorting through some of Dad's tools and boxes of his old Flying magazines. My eyes wandered up to the highest tool shelf, and I froze. There it was. My Top. I just stood there, in utter amazement. "You mean, they kept it?" I thought to myself. Why would Dad keep that thing? He was not that much of a "pack rat." In fact, he was pretty much the opposite. A major purge took place when they had retired and moved to their Cabin at the Lake of the Ozarks, where they lived for many years. Dad was always wanting to clean out the excess "stuff." He may have kept something that really meant a lot to me, but *this*?

I lifted it down from its perch. There was not a speck of dust on it. It looked exactly like it did the moment that I opened its box in 1965. This is weird. I called my sister and my brothers over, and said "Look at this!" My sister was way too young to have remembered it, and even my brothers had to be reminded of that infamous Christmas. I ran in the house with it. "Hey Mom! You never told me you kept this!" I exclaimed. "Well, for Heaven's sake. Where did you find that?" she asked. "In the Garage." "What was it doing there?" "Well, I don't know. I've never seen it before." she said. Now it was getting creepy. Mom reiterated that she did not know how the Top got into the Garage, and that she was sure that Dad probably would not have saved it. She was stumped.

To this day, we're all stumped. How an obscure child's toy from my distant past got onto that shelf in the Garage is anybody's guess. I later found out that this Top is a reproduction of an old American toy, and it's made in China. So it is not my original Top – but I still maintain that it is *exactly* like my Top. The mystery remains as to how it came to be the possession of my parents. Where did it come from and what was it doing there? My Mom certainly didn't know. Anyway, it makes a pretty good story. I now proudly display it on my office shelf, as a memento of that Christmas Eve, 1965. It's not exactly a miracle, but nonetheless, it's pretty weird!

In His Wallet

The year was 1980, and Kansas was on tour again. Touring had become a *very* familiar way of life for us. So much so, that at times it bordered on tedium. It's strange that just a few years before, the very thing that we would have given anything to be able to do, we now found routine. Some of that may be due to the fact that we were touring our latest album, Audiovisions. I have always felt that the album seemed a bit uninspired, compared to its predecessors. Plus, the relationships between the band members had lately been through some trials. There seemed to be a growing distance between us.

I became a Christian on July 25th, 1979, and Dave Hope about a year later. We were riding together in "the Christian car" as we liked to call it. I was still a young believer, and Dave was just a babe. We had experienced some very inspiring and uplifting times since becoming believers, but lately we had encountered some dry and frustrating times. I tried telling Dave that "If the Twelve Disciples ended up giving their lives for their Faith, then why should we expect a bed of roses?" (One new believer searching for the words to comfort another new believer!) Though my statement may be true, it didn't help Dave much. As we were driving along, Dave said, in his distinctive way of joking, "I just wish that we could run into some Christians at the gig tonight, or do an interview or something. You're great, Kerry, but I need some real Fellowship!" "Be careful what you ask, Dave. You may get it!" I replied.

The concert that evening was in Lakeland, Florida. We had played there before, and I always remember liking it. As we pulled up at our Hotel, our Road Manager was there to meet us. He called us over to him, and told us that a large Christian FM Station in Lakeland had called, and wanted us to do an interview. They were willing to send someone in a Van to pick us up after the show, and then drop us off at the Hotel. Dave and I just looked at each other.

"Sure, no problem," I said. True to their word, there was a Van parked behind the Hall after the concert. The Driver was a guy about our age. He said something about being honored to be our Driver, then proceeded to tell us all about this FM Station, and about all the thousands of people that would be listening to our live interview. He said the Station literally could be heard over most of Florida. "Cool," said Dave, and smiled.

The Control Room was pretty impressive, and very professionally run. (As one who has seen hundreds of FM Control Rooms, I know one when I see it.) There was a table set up with Headphones and Microphones for Dave and me. We sat down opposite the interviewers, and were given a bottle of water. Then it began. I asked the host how much time we had to talk, and he said we could talk as long as we wanted to. The "on the air" light went on. After introducing us as members of Kansas, there was some small talk, and, (I seem to remember), they played a track from our new album, probably "Relentless." Then the talk switched to things more Spiritual. Dave and I began with some background details about our lives, and how the band Kansas came to be. We were used to doing this, and had developed a routine. Then they asked me to tell the audience the story of how I came to my faith in Christ. I began talking about my childhood growing up in the Lutheran Church, how I drifted away from it, and my journey through the major religions of the world. I told them how my search for God all came to a conclusion after a concert in Indianapolis in 1979. Then I noticed something strange. Our Driver, who had been standing in the corner and listening to the interview, had a "deer in the headlights" look on his face. He appeared both startled and totally amazed at something. He reached into his jacket and pulled out his wallet.

As I continued speaking, he opened the wallet and took something out. I noticed his hands were shaking. He walked up to the Microphone. The DJ's suddenly looked very nervous – they were thinking about the thousands of listeners, no doubt. The Driver interrupted the interview and said "I'm sorry, but I have something I just have to say. I know this is hard to believe, but I was at that concert in Indianapolis that night. I am holding in my hand the ticket to that concert, that Kansas concert. I have been carrying it with me as a reminder of what happened to me that night. Kerry, I looked up at you on that stage, and all I saw was a soul who was desperately searching for God. I was moved by the Holy Spirit to pray for you. I prayed so hard that I left the concert in tears." The Control Room was silent. I don't know how much "dead air" took place. I was so stunned, I could not speak. Dave asked him "Can I see that ticket stub?" He handed it to Dave, who looked at it for a couple of seconds, and said "Yup, July 24th, 1979, Kansas in Concert." It was at 3:00 the next morning that I gave my life to Christ.

The silence ended when the interviewers began speaking. I had no idea what they were saying, as I was recovering from shock. It was one of those rare moments in which you realize that God is indeed real, and very present with us. Everyone in that room felt it. I was reminded of Dave's statement earlier in the day, "I just wish that we could run into some Christians at the gig tonight, or do an interview or something." The Lord certainly had an answer to prayer in mind for that one, and thousands got to hear it! The Driver took us back to the Hotel. We were all basking in the "Divine Appointment" we had just witnessed. The Driver's story had been a blessing to us, and we had been a blessing to him. A good day on the road.

Afterword

In the interest of maintaining my purpose in writing this book, (chronicling the miraculous events in my life,) I decided to include this final Chapter. It was a hard decision, but not because it is not miraculous. It clearly is. As the character of "Balthasar" in the Movie "Ben-Hur" said, "All life is a Miracle." My hesitancy came because I was unable to write it down. It was so emotionally disturbing to me, that I didn't think I could ever put it into words. I have kept a Diary during certain periods of my life. Many of those early entries were included in "Seeds of Change." However, I stopped writing in it for many years, decades in fact, but (thankfully) started keeping a Computer Diary in February of 2016. I have decided to simply publish my Diary of these events, rather than attempt to write about them. The central theme of this Chapter is Vicci's miraculous (multiple) recoveries. Many people have stories about Cancer, or Heart problems, but very few have both. I have done some editing – mostly the removal of entries that are irrelevant to the theme. There are a few that I have left in that the reader might find interesting. Hopefully, you will find this story as astonishing as I do. I can scarcely believe that my wife lived through it, that I lived through it, and that the rest of my family did as well. It has many ups and downs. Welcome to the Roller Coaster Ride...

8-6-2017 – Last night, as we sat down at the table for dinner, Vicci told me she had found a lump in her breast. I froze. No man should ever have to hear that from his wife. I'm praying.

8-8-2017 – Vicci went to the Hospital and had a Mammogram and a Sonogram done. I would have gone with her, but I still could not bring myself to believe that it was anything serious. The Radiologist said he thought it looked like Cancer. Tomorrow she is getting a Biopsy. I'm still praying.

8-10-2017 – The Biopsy is complete. We still don't know anything.

8-13-2017 – Great Sunday School Class today. Still no word on the Biopsy.

8-15-2017 – The results are in. Adenocarcinoma – Breast Cancer. This is dreadful, but I know the Lord will get us through it.

8-17-2017 – We met with a Surgeon, Dr. Bernsten. She was somewhat encouraging. She is going to remove the Cancer. Vicci may not need Chemotherapy!

8-21-2017 – Today we saw a Total Solar Eclipse. It was cloudy, so we didn't get to see much, except a strange darkness. Hope that isn't significant.

8-22-2017 – We met the Oncologist, Dr. Hashmi. He was rather encouraging also. He told us that the particular type of Cancer that Vicci has is very curable.

8-27-2017 – Went to Church this morning. Lot's of people praying for Vicci.

8-27-2017 – Waiting for Vicci's MRI results.

9-5-2017 – Met with a Reconstruction Surgeon, Dr. Keller, yesterday. Seemed like a nice guy. Described in detail Vicci's upcoming Surgery.

9-8-2017 – They gave us Vicci's appointment for Surgery today. It will be September 21st.

9-16-2017 – Had an appointment with Vicci's Reconstructive Surgeon again today. The Nurse told us all about the post-op procedures.

9-20-2017 – Vicci's Surgery will be tomorrow morning. God's will be done.

9-22-2017 – Vicci came through the Surgery OK, but we got some rather bad news. Unfortunately, two of her lymph nodes were positive. We are waiting for the pathologist's report.

9-25-2017 – Praise God! Her margins were clear. Dr. Hashmi said she still has to have Chemotherapy, however, because of the lymph nodes.

9-30-2017 – Vicci's second Surgery was yesterday. Dr. Bernsten installed a port for her Chemo, and Doctor Keller did more reconstruction. We have to go see him again on Monday. She's facing all this very bravely.

10-1-2017 – Vicci was not able to go with me to Church today. She still has one of the drains in the surgical bra that she has to wear, and she is not able to take a shower.

10-2-2017 – The Doctor gave Vicci a (cautious) good report today, and removed the last of the drains.

10-6-2017 – Today is the North Topeka Arts Center Kansas (Band) event. Vicci has been working very hard on this. I am to play a concert with Kansas, and Vicci has another appointment with the Doctor. John Bowes has agreed to take her to her appointment since I will be at the Concert Hall.

10-7-2017 – The Arts Center event and the Concert went extremely well. It was kind of hard to get in the mood, with Vicci being at the Doctor, but I "burned up" the Guitar on "Wayward Son," even if I say so myself!

10-13-2017 – We saw Dr. Keller again today. Vicci is not healing as well as he expected. We have to dress her wounds twice a day, and if she is not healed up by next week, it could mean another Surgery.

10-18-2017 – Every day I learn more about Cancer, including other side effects or diseases that are *caused* by Cancer. Early this morning I was awakened by the sound of Vicci gasping for breath. She sat on the couch for a while, but it really wasn't getting much better. We called Doctor Keller, and rushed to St. Francis Hospital. After some tests, we found out that she had multiple blood clots, and some fluid on her right lung. This is caused by the Cancer and the installing of her port. What an absolutely demonic disease.

10-20-2017 – We saw Dr. Keller today. Vicci is healing better than he expected, but still has a long way to go. The blood clot issue seems to be under control with her Xarelto prescription.

10-25-2017 – Yesterday we went to the Chemotherapy Orientation as Stormont Vail Cancer Center. Needless to say, Vicci did not enjoy it.

10-26-2017 – Vicci is now on an anti-Estrogen medicine called Anastrozole. Doctor Hashmi says it is nearly a "miracle medicine." It is to prevent a recurrence of the Cancer.

10-27-2017 – Today we saw Dr. Keller again. Vicci's wound is just not healing. We are contemplating another Surgery – a complete Mastectomy. This is probably for the best. Lord help us.

11-8-2017 – Today Vicci had a Mastectomy of her left breast. It was done at St. Francis Hospital. The Surgeons said it went well. I certainly hope so – this is very tiring for me as well.

11-9-2017 – I went to St. Francis to be with her this morning. She was in as good a mood as could be expected. Hopefully I will bring her home this afternoon.

11-13-2017 – Vicci's incision is bleeding. We went to see Dr. Keller yesterday and it was more bad news. She may have to undergo *another* surgery.

11-15-2017 – Today, we took Vicci to Dr. Keller in Lawrence, and he said another surgery was inevitable. They took her downstairs for her 4th surgery at the Hospital in Lawrence. Katy and Becca were there. Dr. Keller thoroughly cleaned the wound, and said it had been infected. He seemed quite sure that she would finally begin healing now.

11-16-2017 – I finished the "Several More Musiks" album and sent it off for manufacturing. It is difficult for me to keep my mind on my music. Vicci is doing OK, but really tired.

11-17-2017 – Vicci is having a really hard time. Now her digestive system is bothering her.

11-18-2017 – She's doing a bit better today, but still tired. One of the nurses called in a new prescription for her. It's hard to keep track of all these pills.

11-20-2017 – Dr. Keller is concerned about the color of fluid in Vicci's surgical drains. He's worried about an E Coli infection.

11-21-2017 – Today we had to take Vicci to a specialist in Lawrence, Dr. Penn. He put Vicci on an IV antibiotic. We have to do this *every day* for at least 10 days.

11-23-2017 – Thanksgiving day! Despite the Cancer ordeal, there is so much to be thankful for.

11-24-2017 – Got a good report from Dr. Keller today. Her incisions are healing nicely!

11-27-2017 – Saw both Dr. Keller and Dr. Penn today. Vicci got her antibiotic infusion, and then Dr. Keller changed bandages and removed one of her drains. They said she is doing well.

12-1-2017 – Today we saw Dr. Keller, and Vicci is at last healing. We don't have to go back for a week!

12-11-2017 – Vicci continues to mend. We see Dr. Hashmi (her Oncologist) on Tuesday. Christmas decorations are up!

12-11-2017 – Well, yesterday I had to go to the Doctor. I was concerned about my blood pressure and fatigue. They gave me an exam, and I appear to be OK. Just stress, I guess. Dr. Borchers agreed. Vicci starts Chemotherapy the day after Christmas.

12-25-2017 – Christmas day today! The kids all came, and we had a great time together

12-26-2017 – Well, today was the big day – Vicci's first day of Chemotherapy. We arrived at the Cancer Center at 10:30, but didn't get underway for an hour. First came a visit with Doctor Hashmi, who authorized her treatment. Next came several nurses, and one who administered the Chemo. All in all, it was pretty painless and surprisingly brief. So far, she feels OK. She even had me stop at a Burger King. She was hungry!

1-2-18 – The Holidays have passed. Kyle and Becca came for New Year's dinner. Vicci has weathered her Chemo Treatment very well – no side effects, Praise God!

1-3-18 – Saw Dr. Bernsten, Vicci's first Surgeon, for a checkup. Had to watch her temperature very carefully today. She was right at the threshold at 100.3.

1-6-18 – Her temperature has been fine the last few days. She made a fine pot of my sisters Taco Soup recipe last night. No side effects from the Chemo!

1-9-18 – Today was Vicci's second Chemotherapy infusion. To-morrow we take her in for her injection of Neulasta, which is sup-posed to boost her White Cell count.

1-14-18 – Had a good day at Church today, although without my wife. Her White Cell count is too low to be in public. She still has no significant ill effects from the Chemotherapy, thank the Lord.

1-16-18 – Vicci had a temperature of 103. I had to take her to the Emergency Room at Stormont Vail Hospital, as her Oncologist in-structed us to do. After a bunch of tests, they admitted her. Her White Cell count was .01! Fortunately, she tested negative for the Flu virus. She is in isolation.

1-17-18 – She is still in the Hospital today. I spent most of the day there with her. She has a nagging cough, which the Doctors say is caused by Neutropenia (low white cells.) We're waiting for her in-jection of Neulasta to kick in so she can come home.

1-18-18 – The very thing I dreaded has happened. Today I woke up with the Flu. I called Vicci and told her the bad news. After con-ferring with Dr. Hashmi, he came up with the following plan. I had to go to a clinic to get an official diagnosis. If it was positive (which after examination the Doctor said I was), I had to bring home a prescription of Tamiflu for both Vicci and myself. Then, when she gets home, I am to wear a viral mask, sleep in a bedroom at the opposite end of the house, frequently wash our hands, and maintain a distance of at least six feet from her. I was willing to comply.

1-19-18 – Vicci did not get home until 6:30 this evening. Kyle went and got her. I am too sick. Did not hear what her White Cell count was, but it must have been sufficient to let her go.

1-20-18 – So far, the Doc's plan is working. I'm very sick, but Vicci has no symptoms. Praying!

1-21-18 – Today is Sunday. The plan is still working. This morning we first watched Charles Stanley, followed by his son Andy. We did this together from opposite sides of the room. I'm feeling marginally better.

1-22-18 – Monday. I'm feeling a bit better. Vicci is still symptom free!

1-23-18 – Today I felt good enough to take her to see Ginger (Oncologist Nurse-Practitioner.) Of course I was wearing my mask. They tested her blood, and her White count was almost normal. Praise God for his faithfulness!

1-26-18 – Still feeling a bit weak and flu-ish, though it has been a week. Vicci still has no symptoms. Tonight I receive the Kansas Native Sons and Daughter's Award, along with Dave Hope.

2-6-18 – Dave and I received the Award. Very nice ceremony, with a large audience. Senator Pat Roberts spoke. He was pretty funny. Vicci is feeling tired from today's Chemotherapy.

2-12-18 – This afternoon Vicci (very graciously) received her 4th Chemotherapy. This completes her Doxorubicin and Cyclophosphamide infusions. Now she moves on to Taxol (in 2 weeks.)

2-16-18 – So far, Vicci still has no side effects.

2-21-18 – Vicci has been in the Hospital for the past two nights, and she will be there again tonight. She has another bacterial infection. She's a bit discouraged, since over a week ago she had her last of the harsh Chemo drugs. This is not a "side effect," but more of the expected variety.

2-24-18 – Today Vicci came home from the Hospital. Praise God!

2-27-18 – Vicci is improving daily. Today we get her blood checked.

3-5-18 – Vicci is still feeling good. She has more Chemo tomorrow. I have been copying old slides to Computer. They are fascinating.

3-7-18 – My first grandson was born today! Lincoln Raymond Livgren was born to Kyle and Becca. Vicci and I went to the Hospital to see him, and the Holder's were all there. (our In-laws) Unfortunately, Vicci couldn't hold him because of her Chemotherapy. She was disappointed.

3-9-18 – They had mercy on her. Vicci got to hold the baby today.

3-13-18 – Vicci got her 2nd infusion of Taxol today. No side effects.

3-20-18 – Today she got her third Taxol treatnent. It's a fine early Spring day.

3-27-18 – Vicci got her 4th infusion of Taxol today. She is doing reasonably well.

4-1-18 – An unusual Easter Sunday. It snowed-sleeted. We went to Church last night instead of this morning. Katy, and Kyle with his family both came over.

4-1-18 – Today Vicci had her 5th Chemotherapy. It's been *really* cold the last couple of days.

4-10-18 – Today we took Vicci to get her Chemo Treatment, but they wouldn't give it to her. She is just too weak, so they delayed it til' next week.

4-17-18 – The 6th infusion of Taxol was today. It went well. Katy is (possibly) buying a house in Kansas City.

4-23-18 – Vicci has her 7th Chemotherapy infusion tomorrow.

4-24-18 – Vicci's 7th Chemotherapy went well. Her blood numbers were good.

4-29-18 – My wife finally got to attend Church with me this morning. She prayed last night that she would feel good enough – and she did. We have to be very careful because her resistance is so weak.

5-1-18 – Vicci's 8th Chemo session was today. She got through it fine, except lately she has been complaining about numbness in her feet.

5-2-18 – Her feet "drove her crazy" last night. Today she called Doctor Hashmi and he prescribed Gabapentin. (the same drug I have to take since my stroke.)

5-8-18 – Today was her 9th Chemotherapy. It went well. 3 more to go. May is here and the weather is beautiful.

5-12-18 – Had a pretty good week. Becca brought little Lincoln over for Vicci to babysit.

5-15-18 –   Today was to be Vicci's 10th Taxol treatment, but it was not to be. As soon as they found out that her hands and feet were numb, they gave her two weeks off to see if it gets better. If it does not, then she is through with Chemo. The Doctor thinks that is enough. If the numbness gets better, or goes away, then she'll do the last three weeks of Chemotherapy.

5-27-18 –   Vicci's 67th Birthday today! We all had Dinner at a Steak House in Topeka.

5-29-18 –   Vicci is through with Chemotherapy. Her body simply couldn't take any more. The Doctor said she was 85% through the treatment, and he seemed pretty confident that it was enough for a good outcome. My prayer is that she gets through this neuropathy she is suffering from, and that it is not permanent. Now the debate begins about whether she should have Radiation.

6-7-18 – Saw Dr. Hashmi today. He placed Vicci into "Survivorship" mode. Praise God! She may no longer have Cancer, but she still has a long way to go to recover from the *treatment*. To complicate things – she fell and has twisted *both* her ankles.

6-12-18 – We have decided not to undergo Radiation Therapy. We met with the Radiation Doctor, who reviewed her case. Vicci's circumstances were borderline, and the minuses greatly outweighed the pluses. She is going to continue to take Anastrazole to prevent a re-occurrence. The Doctors all speak very highly of it. She is in God's hands. Meanwhile, I have completed the first rough mixes of the Cantata. Still many more vocals to record, though.

6-13-18 – Vicci has fallen and broke a bone in her foot. Sigh... Took her to the Emergency Room and they put her leg in a temporary cast.

6-19-18 – After getting her a "Knee-Scooter," she took a spill with it almost immediately. I told her not to "go racing" with it, and not to try to make any sharp turns. What do you think she did? Went racing and made a sharp turn. I hope she didn't hurt her back. A week went by before we had an appointment with an Orthopedic Doctor. They removed the cast and gave her a "boot." She's been getting along pretty well in it.

6-27-18 – Vicci is getting better every day. So am I!

7-1-18 – Had a good Sunday. Vicci came to Church with me in her "boot." Afterward we met Diana Hope, who is here visiting, for lunch. The Bowes' came along.

7-6-18 – Vicci continues to improve. Had the Holder's over for the 4th of July and had a great time. The past few weeks I have been working on my Music collection – just a diversion.

7-17-18 – Yesterday Vicci had her Port (for Chemotherapy) removed. Hooray! Becca and friends and family members came to the house for a swim party. Vicci was tired, so I had dinner with John Bowes and some fans, who were in town.

7-25-18 – Now (of all things) I am dealing with an infection in my right eye. The Doc says it is nothing serious, but it sure is irritating.

8-17-18 – Rob and JoAnn Raynor were here the last 5 days. What a blessing they are.

9-16-18 – Just returned from our trip to visit Vicci's Father in Georgia, (Katy came with us.) He's 91 years old, and just as spry as ever. Had a great time. We got home just in time to babysit our Grandson (Lincoln) starting at 6:30 A.M.!

9-18-18 – I am 69 years old! Had dinner with the kids.

10-1-18 – Another episode. Yesterday (Sunday) Lincoln was dedicated to the Lord in Church. Afterwards, the Holder's, Kyle and Becca, and Vicci and I all went out for Lunch at the Blind Tiger. I ordered the Meat Loaf dinner, which was good and a very ample serving. Being a modest beer drinker, I also ordered a sample of one of their dark beers, (about a shot glass), and a glass of ice water. As I was finishing the Meat Loaf, Brian and I were having an animated conversation about aviation. We were just concluding our lunch, so I reached for my (untouched) glass of cold water, and took a large gulp. Then I finished off my beer, and I immediately felt a sensation of pressure in my esophagus, as if I had attempted to swallow too much. I felt slightly faint. It seemed to me like a second or two passed by, and everyone at the table was staring at me with an expression of alarm on their faces. I had passed out for about ten seconds! Despite my insistence that I was all right, Kyle demanded that I go to the Emergency Room, and everyone agreed, so off we went. Vicci, Kyle and Becca, and Brian and Shelley all went with me. Becca insisted that she saw the Doctor with me to tell her side of the story, and to make sure that mine was right! The Doctor, (Dr. Crider), assumed that I had suffered a T.I A. (mini-stroke.) After listening to my account, which included a previous similar event three years earlier, and after some extensive testing and an E.K.G., she concluded that I had not had a T.I A., but that I had a condition called "Neurocardiogenic Syncope." The good news is that it is avoidable and relatively harmless. (I have to be vigilant in my eating habits, such as drinking more while eating.) However, she told me I must have an Ultrasound scan of my Carotid Arteries since she had heard a "bruit" on my right side while examining me.

10-2-18 – Today I had the Ultrasound Carotid scan. Much to my relief the technician said he saw nothing of concern on my right side. The left side is, of course, completely blocked since my stroke nine years ago. Now I await the opinion of the Doctors.

10-6-18 – Dr. Borchers told me the results of my artery scan. No changes whatsoever since 2009!

10-28-18 – Dennis Greening was out of town, so I taught Sunday School this morning. It went well. Talked about the Dead Sea Scrolls and Halloween!

11-23-18 – Today is Thanksgiving Day. Well, not exactly – it's the day after. The kids are all here and all is well. We have to share them now with the Holder's!

12-19-18 – Vicci had to go to see a Doctor today. She's had Bronchitis for the past week. The Doc examined her and said that she's recovering.

12-23-18 – On the way to Church this morning Vicci began having severe breathing problems. They got worse after we arrived. We had to rush to the Emergency Room. The Doctors examined her, and she has been diagnosed with Heart Failure. This is just hard for me to believe. There is a lot of fluid in her lungs and around her Heart. Lord, please help us.

12-26-18 – I have spent Christmas Eve and Christmas day with Vicci in the hospital. Her Cardiologist, Dr. Gernon, says she is suffering from Cardiomyopathy (damage to the Heart Muscle), most likely caused by the Chemotherapy. The good news is that her Cardiologist says that it is treatable with the proper medications. Also they did a Heart scan today and found absolutely no blockages. She is coming home tomorrow, on our 43rd Wedding Anniversary.

12-28-18 – We finally celebrated Christmas today. The kids were all here.

12-30-18 – The last couple of days have been rough for Vicci. She is pretty weak and tired.

1-1-19 – Vicci feels a bit better today. It's kind of a Roller Coaster ride.

1-5-19 – Well, the Roller Coaster totally derailed. Vicci has been gaining 3-4 lbs. a night for several days, and this morning she couldn't breathe. I took her to the Emergency Room, and they recognized it as Heart failure (again.) They re-admitted her to the Hospital. The Cardiologist, this time Dr. Doyle, said she may be there a while.

1-9-19 – She was released today. Over Saturday night she shed more than 10lbs of water weight! She is feeling much better. She said she is breathing better than she has in *months*. Also, Dr. Doyle all but confirmed that Chemotherapy caused her Heart failure.

1-15-19 – The feeling better didn't quite last. Though, thankfully, her weight has remained stable, she has developed a nagging cough the last 5 days. The Heart Center said this is normal with her

Heart medications, or she has some sort of virus. I am still hopeful, but she is getting very tired of the struggle. We have an appointment with the Heart Center tomorrow.

1-22-19 – Vicci has been struggling with this cough. After they confirmed that it was probably a virus, she has been up and down with it every day. Today she is feeling a bit better. Our daily routine has changed. Every morning when we get up, I get her an Orange or a Banana, and then we sit down to a buffet of pills.

1-23-19 – Vicci is feeling somewhat better this morning. Hopefully this pattern will continue.

1-30-19 – The pattern is continuing! She gets quite tired in the evening, but feels pretty good in the day. Lately I have been working on my Cantata.

2-2-19 – Saw Vicci's Cardiologist (Nurse Practitioner), Emily Bohannon, yesterday. Didn't really tell us anything new. Vicci appears to be (very slowly) getting better.

2-12-19 – Nothing new to report. Vicci is still slowly improving.

2-23-19 – She is definitely feeling stronger – riding our stationary bike once in a while. Answered prayer.

3-1-19 – Vicci has been slowly gaining weight again. This is not good if it's water retention.

3-4-19 – Yesterday morning it snowed, but we went to Church. When we returned home, we had a typical Sunday afternoon. Last night, about 9:45, Vicci fell on the Kitchen floor and was unconscious when I got to her. Her face was lying in a growing pool of blood. As she came to, she couldn't remember what had happened. She had either tripped on a cardboard box that was on the floor, or just passed out. This morning she feels better, but has a couple of black eyes and a swollen nose. We're going to see the Heart Doctor today.

3-5-19 – We went to the Heart Center and saw a Doctor. (Kelsey Jordan) She was not terribly concerned about Vicci's appearance, but she doubled one of Vicci's prescriptions. (Lasix) When we got home Dr. Doyle doubled another one (Metropolol.)

3-6-19 – Vicci lost 4.8 lbs last night!

3-7-19 – Today is Lincoln's 1st Birthday. Vicci has mysteriously gained 7.6 lbs overnight. Crazy.

3-10-19 – Vicci passed out again tonight. After coming to, (she was out about 7 seconds), she insisted that she was all right, and she went to bed. I am taking her to the Hospital in the morning to find out what is going on...

3-11-19 – Again Vicci was admitted to a Hospital Room. A very personable Doctor, Dr. Jesse Vielenthaler introduced himself. He said Vicci was somewhat of a mysterious case. After the mandatory blood test, X-Rays, and two CT Scans, he told us she would be spending at least a couple of days there to find out what's wrong.

3-12-19 – Dr.Vielenthaler, after examining Vicci's chart, told us that he thinks the problem is a combination of things. Her level of Sodium was extremely low, and she had Pneumonia in one of her lungs. Plus, he said she was dehydrated, so he put her on an IV of saline solution. He believes that all three probably resulted in her loss of consciousness. He also ordered a scan of her legs (for clots) and a scan of her Liver.

3-13-19 – Vicci was released to come home today. The tests were all clear, and her Sodium level has come up. Dr.Vielenthaler said not to take her Diuretics (Lasix and Spironolactone) for a couple of days.

3-14-19 – Dr.Vielenthaler has been calling us to see how Vicci is doing. Very nice guy. Vicci lost a couple of pounds last night.

3-15-19 – She gained them back. The Doc says if she gains weight again tomorrow that we should put her back on the Diuretics. Also she is starting to complain a little about being winded.

3-16-19 – We had kind of a rough night. Vicci was having breathing issues, and this morning she had gained two more pounds. (obviously fluid) Earlier, I was about to suggest going to the Emergency Room, but after waking up and giving her the Lasix and Spironolactone, she seemed to feel better. As the day wore on, however, she got a little more "winded." We'll see what the morning brings. Rob and JoAnn Raynor called today. They are always encouraging.

3-17-19 – Had to take Vicci to the Hospital this morning. This time it is more serious. They put her in Intensive Care. Fluid on her Heart, and trouble breathing Oh, Lord...

3-18-19 – It is hard for me to write this. Dr. Doyle ordered her taken by Ambulance to KU's Med Center in Kansas City. He was very wise in doing this. He said her case was beyond his capability. Her Heart is truly failing. He indicated she was going to need some sort of a Heart Pump device. She was admitted to KU's Intensive Care ward, where they have a whole team of Cardiologists looking after her. Katy met me there.

3-18-19 – I am writing this before going to bed. The news is disappointing. Vicci does not qualify for the Heart Pump. Dr. Shah, her new Cardiologist, says her Heart is just too small and weak to accommodate it. To my surprise, (and a little bit of shock), he said her best hope was a Heart transplant. They have begun the whole series of tests she must undergo to prepare her for the procedure.

3-19-19 – Drove to Kansas City to see Vicci at the Hospital this morning. Lots of talk about the Heart transplant. Met several nurses and Doctors. They installed a "Swan" in her right carotid artery. It is a monitoring device. (a long tube is inserted all the way in her Heart.) In addition, they have her on several new Heart meds, among them Melrinone. Seems to make her feel a bit better. More tests today.

3-20-19 – More testing today. Dr. Shah is disturbed that the "Swan" numbers are "too good." He says they don't match up with everything else. Ran into a whole "team" of Cardiologists discussing Vicci in the Hallway. I'm very impressed with this Hospital. Vicci says the Nurses are all great too. I also met a very nice young man named Cliff, who told us everything from A to Z about Heart transplants. They are trying to prepare us.

3-21-19 – More tests done today. They have to test everything, Lungs, Liver etc. They even sent in a Psychiatrist and a Chaplain. Today they did something called a transesophageal echocardiogram (TEE), in order to get a clearer image of her Heart. Also, they had to put in a replacement "Swan." They were convinced that the first one had some sort of flaw.

3-22-19 – Big news! The Heart Transplant is now on hold, for a couple of reasons. First, the Cardiologists have succeeded in getting Vicci's "numbers" leveled out with several different medications. Cliff told us she would be refused for a transplant. Second, the TEE showed that she had a severely leaking Mitral valve. We met Dr. Daon, a Surgeon who is going to attempt to repair it. They don't know yet what effect this surgery will have. Dr. Daon is very hopeful, but Dr. Shah is a bit more skeptical. He says her Heart muscle still must "regenerate." We shall see.

3-23-19 – Just waiting. I do a lot of that lately. Not much happening. This Hospital is kind of a "Ghost Town" on weekends.

3-26-19 – Vicci had her Mitral valve surgery today. It was done with a Laparoscope. Amazing. Dr. Daon said it could not have gone better! The valve went from a "severe leak" to "only a trace."

As for me, I have a feeling that this is going to have a very positive effect.

3-27-19 – Today they did an Echocardiogram.

3-28-19 – Good news! She feels *fabulously* better, and they are moving her to the 4th Floor, awaiting her Defibrillator to be installed. She is all smiles.

3-29-19 – The Defibrillator was put in this morning. The surgeon was Dr. Dendi. No complications. Vicci refers to it as "Dudley," her Guardian Angel.

3-29-19 – They were going to send her home today, but an irregular Heartbeat necessitated another night's stay. My prayer that her Heart information would level out, with no more complications.

3-31-19 – She came home today! I went to Church this morning, then drove to Kansas City and picked her up. Hopefully this time she can stay. We have many instructions about her medications, the Defibrillator, and her incision.

4-3-19 – Here we go again – she's having problems breathing. Doesn't make sense because she felt so great at the Hospital.

4-4-19 – We just got back from KU Med. Much to our relief, Vicci did not have to be admitted again. Dr. Shah, her cardiologist, (with whom we are both very impressed), has readjusted several of her medications. Our collective hope is that this will make her feel much better. She has another appointment on Monday.

4-8-19 – We went to KU again and saw Dana Miller (Dr. Shah's Nurse-Practitioner.) Then we had a meeting with Dr. Daon, (Heart Surgeon), and he dismissed Vicci. All good appointments! Let's hope the meds keep working.

4-10-19 – Vicci's weight is still dropping.

4-13-19 – Today Vicci went to get her nails done, and she hit a post in a parking lot. She damaged her GMC Acadia. Sigh...

4-16-19 – Vicci's water weight has pretty much leveled out for the past 6 days. For instance, yesterdays was 140.0, today it was 141.6.

4-21-19 – Easter Sunday! We both went to Church last night, and the kids all showed up today For the past week or so, Vicci has been pretty stable and feeling good.

4-23-19 – This morning her water weight was up by 3 pounds. Probably due to the Easter dinner. We'll see what tomorrow brings.

4-24-19 – Now her weight was back down to 141.6! Whew!

4-27-19 – Her weight is leveling off. Tomorrow I teach Sunday School – Mark 13:14. Yikes! The Abomination of Desolation.

5-1-19 – Yesterday we went to Kansas City for one of Vicci's appointments. It rained hard all the way there. She had an Echo-cardiogram, and the news was (cautiously) good. The Nurse Practitioner was Dawn Anderson, and she said that though she was not officially trained to read them, that she had seen a lot and that Vicci's Heart looked stronger to her. We celebrated the good news (with Katy) at a very fine restaurant on the Plaza called Eddie V's.

5-2-19 – Today Vicci had her first Cardiac Rehab appointment!

5-7-19 – Vicci saw Dr. Hashmi, her Oncologist, today for a checkup. All clear!

5-14-19 – Yesterday John Bowes called and asked that me meet him at the Blind Tiger Brewery. They had finished making a special beer – "Livgren Lager." It was indeed wonderful. It was dark and very smooth tasting. Kyle, Becca, and Lincoln went with us.

5-21-19 – We went to KC yesterday for Vicci's appointment with her Cardiologist, Dr. Shah. He talked with us quite a bit, examined Vicci, and made some changes in her medications. He removed the Amiodorone, and restored the Metoprolol. Most significantly, he prescribed Entresto, a new Heart failure drug which he spoke very highly of. The (possible) problem is, her blood pressure, though improved, is barely high enough to take it. We're praying.

5-31-19 – Vicci is doing well with the Entresto, though her blood pressure is pretty low, and her weight is still unstable. Nowadays, it seems like all I'm writing about is Medical stuff.

6-3-19 – Today Vicci is struggling again with low sodium level in her blood.

6-5-19 – Vicci continues to gain Heart-related water weight. They made us an appointment tomorrow at KU Med. Here we go.

6-6-19 – Went to KU Med today and saw Dana Miller and Dr. Shah. Katy was there with us. They both examined Vicci and said that her weight gain was (probably) normal! They made some medicine adjustments again, and we were on our way. What a relief!

6-10-19 – Vicci is in the hospital again. A few days ago I drove her to get her hair done. As she was coming out, she suddenly whirled around and lost her balance. She fell against the hood of the car. Scared me half to death. Later, she complained a little about soreness, but we thought no more about it and went to KU Hospital (in Topeka) the next day. On Friday the 7th, she passed out while standing at the Kitchen sink, but she never told me about it. The next day she was having muscle spasms, which were very painful. On Sunday I insisted she go to the Hospital and get it checked out. After X-Rays, they confirmed 3 broken ribs. We can't determine if she broke them when she fell against the car, or later when she passed out.

6-11-19 – She was released today. The Doctors are trying to determine what caused her to pass out. Dehydration, low sodium, low blood pressure, her medications, or a combination. The Doctors who have seen her are Dr, Schroeder, Dr. Dhir (Cardiologist), and Dr. Kaerkmeyer. They changed some of her medications. Reduced her Bumex to one milligram, and are weaning her off the Gabapentin and the Cymbalta.

6-12-19 – Last night Vicci had the longest, and loudest, episode of talking in her sleep. I think I slept about 4½ hours.

6-14-19 – She has been feeling a bit better the last couple of days. I went to the Gym yesterday for the first time in two weeks. Slept very fitfully last night.

6-24-19 – Vicci has been pretty stable. Her weight has been up and down, around 152 lb. Her blood pressure has come up a bit (low 90's to 102), and she's been doing well at Cardiac Rehab.

6-27-19 – Had a close call today. I left my iPhone in a shopping cart at Wal-Mart. I routinely place it in the little tray in the cart since it doesn't fit very well in my pocket. I had loaded the groceries and other stuff into my truck, and made it all the way home, (about 5 miles), before getting that sickening feeling that something important was missing. I raced up our driveway and immediately called the Wal-Mart service desk (on Vicci's phone) and told them my predicament. After waiting about five minutes on the phone, the young lady I had been speaking to told me she had walked out in the parking lot to the spot where I had told her I had left it, and that she had found nothing. I told Vicci "I've got to go back there and find it, if I can." After uttering a silent and desperate prayer, I raced back to the store and went straight to the spot where I had parked, and sure enough, no iPhone. I went inside to the service desk and told the nice young lady, (whose name was "Kerri" by the way), that I was the guy who had lost his phone. She took my information, and as I was about to walk away she said "You might check the cart receiving area to see if it is there." I

175

knew where that was, by the entrance. I took one look, and my Heart sank. There was more than a hundred carts there, in three long rows, all jammed together. The odds of my finding it were pretty dim. I walked down the first row – nothing. I couldn't even see into the center row, so I gave that up. I was just about to give up when I recognized a dark shape about a dozen carts into the third row. My phone! It was not easy to get to, believe me. Those carts were really wedged in there, but I got it out. On the way home, with a satisfied smile on my face, I thanked the Lord for watching out for the little, insignificant things in our lives, as well as the truly important things.

7-1-19 – Now we are dealing with withdrawal from Cymbalta. Other than weaning Vicci off of it (two weeks at half a dose), the Doctors never said anything about what to expect. Two days ago, she was as sick as I had ever seen her, or *anyone* for that matter. Severe headache, and absolutely gripped with nausea. She was throwing up so hard that I came within a hair of calling an ambulance. She is doing better today.

7-4-19 – We had (sort of) a quiet 4th of July. First time I never bought any fireworks. Rob Raynor's daughter and her family (4 kids) visited us, and later Kyle, Becca, and little Lincoln showed up. Vicci is feeling much better.

7-12-19 – Man, this is embarrassing, especially after relating the story about how I had lost my iPhone, and then recovered it. I have lost it again! I was in my ATV, spraying weeds in our front pasture. My phone was in my pocket. Somehow it fell out, I know not where, in the middle of 76 acres of very tall grass. Vicci and I went back and forth in the field for about an hour, trying to call my phone (from hers), in the hope that we would be able to hear it ringing. After realizing that wasn't going to happen, I raced to the store and purchased a new one. (iPhone 8.) I really was not that concerned, since I had recently backed up my old iPhone 5 on iTunes. I got home and plugged it into the computer and it said "this iPhone can not be recognized on this computer." Needless to say, *then* I got concerned. After exhausting all my computer skills, I finally found the solution at 4am. (well, sort of) I had to purchase software from a British website that would extract the backup from iTunes. (iPhone Backup Extractor) The software worked beautifully, recovering all texts, photos, contacts, etc., but I spent the next day manually entering all my contacts in the new phone. The moral of the story – keep an eye on your cell phone!!

7-17-19 – Vicci had an appointment at KU to have her Heart checked today. Hard to believe, but all was well! Had dinner afterwards with Katy at Eddie V's.

7-18-19 – KU Med called today to tell us that Vicci's Potassium level was really high. They told us to suspend her Spironolactone for a week. She has been feeling queasy.

7-19-19 – Today Vicci was really sick all day. I did not know that the level of Potassium in one's body can do that.

7-20-19 – Today she felt somewhat better. Still a bit queasy.

7-28-19 – Had a pretty good Sunday. Didn't make it to Church, just Sunday School, but Dennis Greening is an awesome teacher. Vicci has been feeling much better.

8-6-19 – Vicci is still feeling good, praise God! Becca and Lincoln came home yesterday, and spent the day with us. I recorded a guitar track in the studio.

9-7-19 – Made a trip to KU Med yesterday for Vicci's appointment with Dr. Shah. As usual, Katy met us there. All was well, except for an elevated Potassium level. She has been doing pretty well the last couple of weeks. Had lunch afterwards at Houlihans.

9-9-19 – Vicci began eating Oatmeal every morning (per Doctor's instructions.) She would say Yuck! I cooked it for her. She pretends she doesn't like it. (In truth, she thinks it's OK, but doesn't want to admit it!)

9-17-19 – Well, she fell again and blackened her eye. She got up to go to the bathroom (too rapidly) and lost her balance. I don't believe this was a "Heart thing." Her sense of balance has been messed up by the Chemotherapy. Someday they have got to find a different way of dealing with Cancer. The cost of "side effects" is (almost) not worth it.

9-18-19 – I have now been alive for 70 years!

9-25-19 – Vicci has been (slowly) recovering the past week. I have been shopping unsuccessfully for a Motorhome (before we take our upcoming trip to Georgia.) I have also been practicing "Dust in the Wind" for the Kansas Concert on the 4th. Hard to believe I have to practice that song. Having had the stroke makes it the most difficult song for me, due to the weakness of my right hand.

10-3-19 – "Dust" has been driving me crazy. I just can't play it like I did before. I have had to invent a new finger-picking technique to accomplish it.

10-4-19 – Played with Kansas tonight at the Topeka Performing Arts Center. It went surprisingly well. It was great to see all my old (and new) friends again.

11-23-19 – This morning I am still stunned. Yesterday was Vicci's appointment at KU in Kansas City to have her Heart tested and evaluated. It has been established that her Heart was severely damaged by Chemotherapy, and she was previously diagnosed with Heart Failure. Her "Ejection Fraction" had been 10-15, almost too low to live. My hope was that we would get a reading of 20-30, enough to escape a Heart transplant. Normal is 50-55. After her test, her Cardiologist, Dr. Shah, kept staring at the screen, saying "Completely normal! Beautiful! Look at this. This is a normal Heart!" The Ejection Fraction was 53! We were amazed, and clearly so was the Doctor. Her Heart is normal, but this is not normal. It is quite extraordinary, perhaps even miraculous. Praise God for His intervention!

3-2-20 – We just returned from KU Medical Hospital for another Heart checkup and Echo-Cardiogram. Doctor Daon (Surgeon) released Vicci from treatment. She has one more appointment with her Cardiologist, and I expect he may do the same. In any event, this is good!

8-12-20 – The appointment was delayed because of the Coronavirus Pandemic, but we saw Dr. Shah today. He examined Vicci, and said we don't need to see him for a year!

The End

Thus ends this book. Believe it or not, I have many more miraculous events I could write about, but I just can't include them all.
May you all find the miracles in your own lives. Look for them, for
they are surely there, and especially the greatest miracle of all –
God's Love and provision for Mankind.

2880 Mulvane, Home of the Livgrens

Kerry with the "Dust in the Wind" Guitar, 2020

"The Gimlets" and Bill Foster, St. Joseph, Missouri

My Top

Schloss Kronberg, 1978

My Uncle Ole and his invention, The "Ole-Vox"

Vicci on Maui before we boarded the ill-fated Sailboat

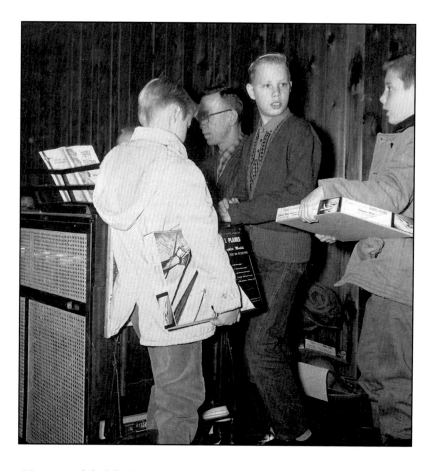

Kerry with his Dad at the Goodyear Christmas Party, 1959

Famed "Yardbirds" Will Perform Here

Coming to Emporia Wednesday night will be a nationally popular recording group, "The Yardbirds," top British exponents of the "rave-up" sound for the Epic Company.

The Yardbirds will play at Renfro's, 1114 East Sixth Ave. The stop in Emporia is part of a national tour that began in Chicago Friday. After leaving here, they will go to Iowa, Texas and Washington before arriving in Hollywood for personal appearances on nationally syndicated television programs. They will appear on "Shivaree," "Never Too Young," "The Lloyd Thaxton Show" and "Where the Action Is."

Their current hit, "I'm a Man," is their third best-seller in a row.

Newspaper Clipping about the Yardbirds playing in Emporia, Kansas, 1965

Kerry and his Cessna, 1980

Vicci receiving Chemo, 2018